the author

Mother of four grown children and now grandmother to four, Michele estimates she has also helped raise nearly a thousand children throughout her thirty-six-year teaching career. She has taught and/or coached in a variety of positions, in dozens of different schools, in three states in the USA, in New Zealand and in Canberra, Australia. She credits her professional longevity and joy to her sense of humour and her appreciation for the marvellous diversity of young personalities. She currently teaches kindergarten in Canberra, Australia and enjoys sharing her stories with her husband Peter and her extended family.

TEACH ON!

Michele Hillory

TEACH ON!

Vanguard Press

VANGUARD PAPERBACK

© Copyright 2020
Michele Hillory

A CIP catalogue record for this title is
available from the British Library.

ISBN 978 1 784658 74 8

Vanguard Press is an imprint of
Pegasus Elliot Mackenzie Publishers Ltd.
www.pegasuspublishers.com

First Published in 2020

Vanguard Press
Sheraton House Castle Park
Cambridge England

Printed & Bound in Great Britain

Dedication

For my husband, Peter, who also was a teacher
once upon a time,
and my Grandma Bessie, who taught in a one room
schoolhouse in Colorado in 1912.

Acknowledgements

I would like to thank my husband, Peter, for encouraging and believing in me as I struggled to bring my scattered and disjointed stories together into a book while teaching primary school full time. Thank you to Vicky and the team at Pegasus Publishing, for making it happen.

I also want to thank my children, Ben, Katira, Hillory and Luke and their partners, Natalie, Grady, Daniel and Stephanie, for joining me on this journey by reading my manuscripts, laughing at my stories and providing brutally honest suggestions. I am grateful to my daughter, Katira, for her extensive final edits and my daughter, Hillory, for her fun cover design.

My grandchildren, Thomas, Henry, Willa and Allegra, kept me balanced.

Other early readers included my mother, Mimi, father, Ben, lifelong friend, CeCe and colleague, CJ, who all gave me advice and hope. I'd also like to thank my parents for teaching me to tackle challenges (like writing a book) with determination, persistence and a sense of humour.

I credit my five siblings, Dan, Marty, John, Benj and Andy, and several dozen cousins for developing my tolerance for chaos and the ensuing resilience that it takes to be a teacher.

I also give my heartfelt appreciation and love to all of the children that I have had the joy of teaching over the years. You are the reason I teach. You keep me young, challenge my brain and make me laugh every day. My story is your story.

Forward

As my book nears publication, education systems worldwide have suddenly been thrown into chaos by an aggressive little virus called Covid-19. Parents all over this planet are being asked to take on a larger role in teaching their children as families are asked to self-isolate at home. I think I speak for teachers all over the world when I say that we teachers have and are working hard to create online programs that minimize family stress levels. However, there is a world of difference between the expectations (real or perceived) put on parents through this temporary online schooling and traditional home schooling.

Home schooling is normally a choice that parents make. They decide for a variety of reasons that they will teach their own children at home. Whether they buy a curriculum or create their own based on the government standards, they have chosen to take responsibility for the education of their children. During Covid-19 teachers retain the responsibility for the education of the children enrolled in our classes. Teachers are creating and conducting online lessons from their own homes while quite possibly also teaching and caring for their own kids. As such, some teachers may feel that parents need to realise that whatever they are going through right now (while guiding their children through prearranged lessons delivered by teachers via video) it is nothing compared to what we do on a daily basis with a couple of dozen or more students in the classroom.

There is a serious flaw in this reasoning. We are trained as teachers and parents are not. I look at it this way: if a parent feels anxious about being asked to be a teacher, it may be comparable to asking me (a sixty-four-year-old veteran teacher) to just put out a house fire with a fire hose I don't have the strength or training to hold and point in the right direction. To make an additional extreme analogy based on another of my own offspring's occupations, it might be like asking me to just do one little stunt. Just jump out of this car and tuck and roll – just this once. Asking parents to temporarily be teachers whilst still doing their own job from home IS a challenging experience despite the lifeline we are throwing them.

Once we teachers ironed out the glitches and began to create video lessons from home, we discovered a few silver linings for the education profession from this annoying pandemic after all. First and foremost was the ability to mute students. This little perk was invaluable when holding live Google meets with a couple of dozen kindergarteners, all chattering at once.

Next, teachers like me who have been teaching for more than three decades increased our limited tech skills exponentially. Through the magic of video, we could reshoot a botched lesson. Blissfully unaware of whether kids understood or not, we could plow through a lot of curriculum. All joking aside, this lack of feedback and personal interaction created major stumbling blocks to learning.

Despite this quite obvious flaw to online learning, I do want to mention one more tiny upside to teaching from home. It was delightful to be able to pee whenever I wanted and to eat lunch without interruption.

As they have supported their children through this home learning journey, parents have begun to understand that educating their little darlings is a mixture of fun, aggravation, love, frustration and discovery. It is exhausting, exhilarating, challenging and joyful all at the same time. Teachers know this. It is our wonderful and rewarding reality.

For me personally, due to the power of shared experience, a few more people might be interested in reading *Teach On!*

Introduction

I am not an expert, nor have I won any major educator awards, done any formal research, or earned a PhD, but over the course of my thirty-six-year teaching career I have taught and/or coached in a variety of positions, in dozens of different schools, in three states in the USA, in New Zealand and in Canberra, Australia. I have been a full-time classroom teacher at every grade level from kindergarten to sixth grade and I have even taught eighth grade science. I have also taught as a specialist at the elementary school level in Science, PE, Reading Recovery and other challenging roles. So, that definitely makes me experienced, and gives me the right to spout off to some degree about my chosen profession, in particular because I still love teaching.

A few years ago, I would have said without a doubt in my mind that teaching Physical Education was my favourite gig, but after teaching first grade for a few years and now teaching kindergarten, I have been completely won over by those little knee-knockers. Teaching five and six-year olds gives PE a serious run for its money.

However, after a few years even those tiny cherubs can start to wear you down. "Why?" you beseech them.

"Why are you literally crying over spilled milk? Does it really truly matter what colour straw you got? Why do you care that Joey just called you a poo poo-head? What is a poo-poo-head anyhow?"

Honestly, I believe the trick to teacher longevity is to keep moving. If you sit in one position too long moss can start to grow on one side of your head and fog up your brain. Move on. Branch out. Step out of your comfort zone. You don't have to change schools, or towns, or countries as I have, but for pity's sake don't stay in the same room, teaching the same grade level and the same things for thirty-five years. Seriously, nobody needs to know how to use a slide-rule any more.

Being a teacher was never my lifelong dream. I wanted to be a farmer. I had earned a Bachelor's Degree in Horticulture and was working as the manager of the green plant division of a large greenhouse firm in Oregon that specialized in cut roses when I decided to go back to university to become a teacher. One of my favourite duties at the greenhouse was to take school groups on tours and it was while saying goodbye to one of those delightfully inquisitive groups of children that I decided to make a career change. It may have been an irrational decision based on the desire to have a more lengthy conversation than was possible with roses, or those who had been cutting them for forty-two years, but it turned out to be a good one.

I earned my Bachelor's Degree in Education when our oldest son was a baby and finished my Masters in

Education when the youngest of our four kids was an infant. FYI – earning a Master's Degree while raising four children under the age of six is not a recommended course of action no matter how marvellous your husband may be.

If you ask prospective teachers why they want to teach, invariably they smile indulgently and emphatically declare, "Because, I like kids." Of course they do. Don't we all. But, as a retired principal friend of mine once pointed out, that is not reason enough to build a career on, because we are not always going to like the kids. Honestly no self-respecting teacher is going to readily admit it, but much as we always *love* the kids, we do not always *like* them. This is because they are not always likeable. To be honest, neither are we.

So, why do I teach? It is not because I have any illusion that I will change the world, nor is it for the summers off (which is not strictly true anyhow) and it certainly is not for the money. After some self-reflection I have concluded that I am still a teacher after all these years because the kids make me laugh every day. Honestly – every day!

This book is my own take on teaching, told through my personal journey. It is not meant to be a textbook. Nor are any of my 'reality-check' stories meant to scare anybody off of this fabulous profession. Hopefully my stories serve as a window into the real-life world of a teacher. Whether you are a teacher, used to be a teacher, want to be a teacher, are in a relationship with a teacher, or simply hope to understand a teacher, this book is my humble gift to you.

I am currently educating pint-sized munchkins again as a kindergarten teacher in Australia and I plan to continue teaching until I am too old to see the humour in a fart. But while my humour is still intact it is time to tell my story. If this is the first book you have read about teaching, I have two things to say to you. First, good luck if this will be your primary source of information. Second, don't even think about teaching if you don't have a sense of humour. Drop the chalk and back away now.

Drop the chalk in any case, because you won't find a chalkboard.

Teach on!

First Impressions

The first day of school each year is the time when the kids and teacher size each other up. It is a bit like when two proud mommies push their little babies face to face in their prams. The infants eye each other up and down. They make lame attempts to communicate. They make a face or two. Invariably they unintentionally end up making each other cry.

Veteran teachers are full of contradictory advice on how this first encounter should be approached. There is the old American adage of, "Don't smile before Thanksgiving," presumably meaning you want to be ornery enough the first couple of months to scare the kids into good behaviour. The flip side of this method is to be all fun and games for the first couple of weeks in hopes that the students will consider you to be their new best friend and be fooled into thinking that they will play their way through the third grade. Regardless of which end of the spectrum you choose to operate from, your students and fellow staff will have a first impression.

But before you get too worried, remember that first impressions are not etched in stone. Chances are the kids might remember that first day, but if it didn't go well children are a lot more forgiving than their grown-up counterparts. If your charges are under the age of eight all you have to do is smile. It's magic. You are their teacher and they are in love. As they get older they do get a bit more discerning. Greeting sixth graders at the door with a puppet talking in silly voices is not likely to score you any points, whereas if you take that same puppet into kindergarten you have a winner.

It is not just the students who are forming first impressions. Your colleagues also check you out when you are the 'new kid on the block' and I have been the new kid more than anybody else I know. The mid-year start is the roughest. Massive loads of catch-up are required just to get up to speed on curriculum, procedures, expectations, etc. Meanwhile every colleague and student introduces him or herself and expects that you will remember their name a full thirty seconds later.

I was clueless as to the nature of the school community my first day (mid-year) of relief teaching in Australia. The principal came by to welcome me at the outside door to my classroom as I was ushering the students in. As I turned to say hello to her I continued pulling the sliding door closed with my arm behind me. Perhaps predictably, I managed to crunch an adorable little girl's head in the door. Oops! What an awesome first impression for both the kid (who literally had an impression on her head) and the principal.

To my astonishment, the principal shrugged it off with an odd little grin as I swung around to apologise to the stunned child. However it did not take long in that classroom, in the presence of that freckle-faced, redheaded, spawn of the devil to realise that the principal probably had a secret desire to slam that particular child's head in a door herself.

I'm convinced that this particular principal probably would have always remembered me after the skull-denting incident, but I solidly cemented myself in her memory with a comment I made later that same day in the staff lounge. I am not sure what came over me. Perhaps I was still a little bit emboldened with the fact that I had made a pre-emptive strike at a child that I had grown to despise in less than three hours and apparently also received unspoken approval from the principal.

Whatever the reason, we (the principal, several other teachers, and myself) were in the staff lounge having lunch when a very small child knocked and asked if he could get a drinking glass for his teacher. As the child reached unsuccessfully for the shelf the principal, who was all of five feet nothing herself, hopped up and got it down for him. She smiled at him, patted him on the head and soothed, "I have trouble reaching things myself sometimes." To which I quipped, "Yes. But, he will grow out of it." There was a pause in conversation – during which time I was pretty sure this was my first and last day of relief teaching at that school – followed by laughter all around and several years of regular work at that school.

My first full time teaching position in Australia came out of the blue one day when I was called to take over a Year Two class just a couple of weeks into the school year. The teacher had just up and quit one day. That should have set off some alarm bells in my head. The reason for this abrupt departure became apparent within an hour or so.

This school was located in a rough area where attendance was an ongoing issue, swearing routine and discipline a constant challenge. As I warily entered that empty and eerily quiet classroom on my first day I found that it only contained thirty-two little student desks, a teacher desk and an out of date pull-down map of the world as it looked before the Cold War. Somebody had cleaned the place out.

As I stood in that barren room I realised that in my experiences as a long-term contract teacher I had always had at least some sort of guidance as to what the class had been learning. I scrounged around a bit looking for clues. Perhaps there was a copy of the departing teacher's lesson plans, some books or even some recent student work – anything that might give me a hint as to what the kids had done the first couple of weeks and what direction they were headed. Nothing. No joke. There was nothing at all in the room.

So, I headed back down the hall to ask the principal what the deal was. Trying in vain to stifle the lingering shreds of my American accent I broached the subject of curriculum. The conversation went something like this.

"Excuse me, sir, but there is nothing in my classroom."

"As in?"

"Well I was hoping you might have a curriculum or something for me to follow."

"Do you need one?"

"Well, I guess not," I said, backing slowly out of his office.

"OK then. On with it then."

"Good talk, sir."

Boy, did I ever give him a memorable first impression. I just visualized him shaking his head and thinking, "Spoiled American with her basal readers and structured curriculum."

I made a slightly better first impression on the kids. I went to the supply room and got paper, pencils, markers, paint and chalk and we made murals for the walls and started a class learning journey story. We went outside and collected stuff for a science table and had our first class run. The 'field' we ran around was dried up and full of broken glass and the kids were panting after about fifty meters. Somehow they all completed one lap and returned my high fives with grudging enthusiasm. Tough crowd, but we were on our way. I was not naïve enough to believe that they would be pudding in my hands, but at least I wasn't going to be steamrolled and quitting after the first couple of weeks. Score one for me.

By the end of the day I felt we were all really beginning to connect as a group on some very basic primal level. As I gathered everybody together on the floor for a quick debrief before dismissal I asked if anybody had any questions. One little guy raised his hand and asked, "Miss? Could you tell us your name?" Oops.

My first full time job in the USA was a much easier ride. I was in my new job as a Physical Education teacher for less than a week when compliments began to pour in from other teachers and the parents at the school. Not just compliments, but over-the-top effusive diatribes on how awesome I was. I was baffled. How could any of these people know what sort of teacher I was after only a few days unless I was under some sort of covert surveillance? Even then I am not sure my teaching had been of the quality that would evoke such enthusiasm. Not that I was insecure or anything, but it all began to make me a little nervous. Had I been transported into some sort of alternate universe where negativity was banned and extreme confidence boosting was mandatory?

A chance encounter in the staff lunchroom began to shed light on my situation. I ate lunch one day with a regular substitute at the school who asked me who I had replaced. When I told her I had replaced the PE teacher she literally clapped her hands together, clutched them to her chest and breathed, "Thank God the children are free of that tyrant." Apparently I was replacing the last remaining member of the Gestapo and the community was so relieved that they couldn't help but shower me with goodwill.

One day just a week or so later I was accidentally beaned in the head with a ball while the fifth graders were playing a game. It didn't knock me down and cause little birdies to tweet around my head or my eyes turn to Xs like in the cartoons, but it did cause my head to deviate from its position and made quite a loud smacking noise as it hit.

The gym went silent. Nobody spoke and nobody moved. When I began to laugh the class let out their collective breath in a massive sigh of relief. Lifting my hands palms up and shrugging my shoulders I said, "What? It was an accident. Relax."

One youngster stammered, "Well, it's just that, just that, well, we thought we were dead."

I gently worked on their PTSD over the next few weeks.

Unfortunately, what you wear and what you drive (as all commercial advertising will try to tell you) inevitably becomes a part of those first impressions. I am severely lacking on both counts. As a family we never owned a new car. This would not normally be an obvious standout in a teacher parking lot except that we as a family took 'used car' to a whole new level.

In Colorado I drove a twenty-seven-year-old Ford Explorer that looked as if it was made of tin foil that had been crumpled and flattened back out. That's because that is exactly what happened. A deer jumped into it. No, you heard right, a deer *jumped into it* knocking off the side mirror and smashing in the driver's side door. Our local mechanics pounded it back out for us, but it was not smooth. The matching passenger side crumple was compliments of unknowns in a parking lot. I never had trouble spotting my car.

During a brief stint back in Minnesota when our kids were very young, I was driving a $1.00 (that's right, one dollar) Volvo with no floorboards in the front. If you happen to have lived in the northern regions of the USA back in the 70s and 80s when they used salt on icy roads you know all about rusted out floorboards. I generally warned any front seat passengers in advance to not lift up the rubber floor mat, so as to avoid the piercing shriek when they noticed the road roaring past through the gaping hole.

The back seat area (where there was still a floor) was so disgusting that I threatened our kids if any object belonging to them touched the floor I would burn it. They knew that was an immediate possibility since steam and smoke billowed from the engine region whenever the car was running. Eternal damnation for any toys left on the car floor was not a big stretch for their fine-tuned imaginations. The purchase price of one dollar explains the rest of the condition of the car.

Anyhow, I had managed to score a few inte
for full time teaching jobs and had to rely on the
to get me there. The problem was my time management
has never been great. On top of that I needed to stop
approximately every five miles to add a gallon jug of
water to the radiator.

In addition, upon arrival I didn't want the
administration to call emergency services as I pulled
into the parking lot in a cloud of smoke, so I usually
parked a block or so away and ran into the interview
trying to suppress my slightly wild-eyed and frantic
expression. We returned to Australia within six months
without me successfully landing full time work.

The family van we had in Australia when the kids
were growing up was not much better. This one had
actual floors and nifty geometric designs made of blue,
green and orange triangles, circles, and squares painted
on its silver sides. However, the Silver Bullet as we
fondly referred to it, had one rather major flaw in that it
didn't start with any kind of predictable regularity. If
other people were travelling with me (as in a husband or
scrawny-legged children) it was not a big issue because
it had a nice rear hatch door feature and was a manual
shift, so the passengers would push it until the driver
could pop it into gear and then the pushers would leap
into the back, pull down the hatch, scramble over the
seat backs and buckle in.

When you arrived at your destination it was best to
remember to park on a hill, because taking off the

parking break and rolling down the hill was a much more efficient way to start the car than all that running and pushing. Unfortunately, hills are not a feature of most school parking lots.

During the life of the Silver Bullet we had a driveway that sloped steeply down to our carport that (oddly enough) had a garage door on it. One evening I proudly related a story of triumph to my husband. The Silver Bullet had been parked in the driveway about two meters from the garage door. Naturally it wouldn't start that morning when I got a late call to relief teach and the kids were all off to school already. To add to the fun it was raining.

Boldly I decided that since I was pretty good at the downhill roll start, I would most certainly be able to successfully take off the brake, disengage the clutch, let it roll and pop it into gear before hitting the garage door. I would have a go at it.

Astounding myself, I managed this feat flawlessly, with the engine sputtering to life as I slammed on the brake with about an inch to spare. After allowing the engine to settle down, I then used the handbrake to ease my way back up the driveway, never so much as touching the garage door.

As I finished my heroic story, my dear husband patted me on the back, congratulated me and then asked why I hadn't simply opened the garage door and given myself the length of the carport to roll. Well, I just don't know the answer to that.

The other painfully attention-grabbing feature of this vehicle was that when you stopped and turned the engine off it rumbled quietly for a few seconds, coughed a little bit and then let out an explosive bang that was akin to a commercial-grade firecracker. It was far less embarrassing to just ride my bike to school. So like my van pushing children, I developed quite a good fitness base just getting to and from school each day.

I digress. Getting back to the first impressions issue. My poor fashion sense is all my own doing. I have never had a good eye for it. When I was a young girl I would walk out of my bedroom proudly dressed to go somewhere and my mother would just wordlessly twirl her finger in a circular 'go back' motion and I would go back and try again.

I taught PE for the first four years that we lived in the USA, so I could handle that dress code. As my girls grew older though, they began to make sure my closet did not contain anything too embarrassing. It helped that I took no offense at this remediation. When they went off to university I had to rely on my defective fashion instincts again. Now that I am over sixty years old and not obligated to even pretend to be cool, as long as I don't wear a miniskirt or a housedress, I feel I am somewhere in the ballpark. It has always made sense to me (especially when teaching in the primary grades) to wear clothes that I didn't care too much about since paint, markers, food and snot tend to be magnetically attracted to clothing. I try to strike a balance between comfortable/casual and bag lady.

I also have freaky long legs, so skirts and shorts that look adorable on some of my younger colleagues look wildly inappropriate on me. I do not wear high-heeled shoes to school. I am quite fascinated with the women who do teach in heels. They totter around precariously during recess duty on icy basketball courts trying to corral wayward children without breaking their necks. Their back, feet and ankles hurt relentlessly. Yet they persevere in the name of fashion. I will not at any point in my career wear high-heeled shoes to school. It's an easy vow to keep, since I don't own any.

Thankfully with intensive fashion therapy from my daughters and some carefully guided purchases, I can now proudly say that I own two pairs of pants that are not jeans, a couple of fun skirts and some tops that are not printed with the name of a 10 km race.

Even once you begin to feel like your public image is reasonably stable it can still be altered by incidents beyond your control. Perhaps this is why one of my first graders left a non-committal note on my desk a couple of weeks into a new school year. Bedecked with hearts and rainbows it read, "I love you miz daviz... so far."

So, my advice on the first impression thing:

1. Wear middle-of-the-road clothes. Don't look like you are attending a wedding, but don't wear the stuff you wore on the weekend while refinishing the back deck.

2. Don't slam anybody's head in a door. That only works if others harbor a secret desire to harm that particular child.
3. Try to replace somebody that nobody liked.

Real Kids

Twenty-six young cherubs are sitting cross-legged on the carpet in front of my chair demonstrating their best 'whole body listening'. They are gazing intently at me with undivided attention, hanging on my every word. Right. Of course they are. We all have a right to dream.

Mental imagery is a powerful tool in mastering doubt and fear of the unknown. Your carpet-sit image most likely will be serene, orderly and heartwarming if you have just finished your teacher training and you are filled to the brim with hope and anticipation. It's the ultimate dream. Hold on to it tightly. It won't take long for the true nature of the beast to emerge. That, my friend, is what makes this profession so interesting.

The picture that pops into my head when doing this little exercise is not exactly serenity. It is based on flashbacks to a challenging first grade class of twenty-six real kids that I had in the USA several years ago and it goes more like this.

Only the front row of children is sitting cross-legged at my feet with rapt attention. Their 'hands-up' arms are twitching in anticipation of the first opportunity to show off snippets of an impressive six years of accumulated knowledge. Near the back of the group, two kids are whispering to each other, apparently oblivious to the fact that I can see them. Another three are absent-mindedly unravelling bits of their socks, shoelaces, or the edge of the carpet. One boy is picking his nose, examining the extracted substance and meticulously ingesting it. Two giggly girls are taking turns playing with each other's hair. A couple of eyes-to-the-front boys are surreptitiously slipping trading cards to each other. One little guy is sneaking tiny bites of Pringles from a stash of the salty snack in his front hoodie pocket. Sitting right beside him, a hungry classmate is gobbling up the crumbs from the carpet. A couple of sporty kids are picking dried recess mud from the treads of their athletic shoes. Hungry Boy seems unperturbed when he occasionally pops a nugget of mud into his mouth instead of the Pringle remnants.

Meanwhile off to the side a bit, a child surely on the spectrum, although undiagnosed, is busy soothing herself by flapping paper strips in front of her face. An intrigued classmate is trying to imitate the flapper's intricate hand movements. Another little cherub is spinning his head slowly around like a wobbly top about to tip over, quite obviously relishing the dizzy sensation.

Through it all, Prissy Perfect sits near the back, slowly shaking her head, judging me for my lack of follow through. Get over it kid. Who is to say some of your peers are not currently multi tasking, which just might bring my student engagement rate up above 80%, a perfectly acceptable rate in my book.

This particular group of kids nearly drove me into early retirement. Luckily like most professional athlete 'retirements', the move didn't stick and I was back in the mix within a couple of months.

Kids are not mini adults. We all know that. Sometimes they may display some mildly bizarre behaviours that could seem disturbing if you have not encountered them before. Two of the children described above had official diagnoses of ADHD and ASD. Those diagnoses may even have been legitimate. However, I feel teachers should know that a primary school child could display any of the behaviours described above and still be a very typical child.

To be perfectly honest, some of these behaviours can persist well into high school and beyond. If a person does actually outgrow or learn to hide these behaviours, they will undoubtedly resurface in the eighth or ninth decade of life. One of my sisters, who has spent the past thirty-plus years working as a registered nurse with the elderly in aged-care facilities, has confirmed that my hypothesis is correct. In fact, when she and I begin to tell funny stories to entertain each other, the antics of our charges are alarmingly similar.

Here is just a small sampling of a few classics:

Puppy dog – As the name suggests, this is the persistent and unrelenting shadowing of your every move by another living creature. Driven mostly by the desire to be close to you, this behaviour can also involve factors such as: busy-body tendencies, an expectation that you may drop something edible or salvageable, to distract you from your mission, or to stalk and murder you. Whatever the reason, if you are not careful when reversing direction you could tread on the child behind you.

Staring – This mostly has to do with an age-related lack of inhibition. The mesmerized child sees something unusual (like a new teacher) and stops in her tracks and just stares. If the object of her hyper-attention is fascinating enough, she will have a slack-jawed, glassy-eyed look about her and not even a meteorite landing on the playground right next to her will break the stare.

Hugging – Sometimes unsolicited hugs can come at you fast, furious and out of context. Some of these kids may engage in bone crushing bear hugs about your unsuspecting knees. Others just saunter on over and slip their arms around your leg or middle while you are talking to somebody else. Child behaviour analysts sometimes try to tag the hug-attackers as craving affection because they have too little or too much affection in their life. In my experience, excessive hugging usually seems to be more of a personal preference thing. I am a hugger. As I see it, once a hugger – generally always a hugger.

The sway – If you were lucky enough to have honed your funny bone on the TV humour of the early 70s, you will remember a *Laugh-In* character called Edith Ann. Lily Tomlin's portrayal of a pig-tailed child in an oversized rocking chair was spot-on. Edith Ann never sat still in. She rocked, and swayed and wriggled in that rocking chair as she babbled on about nothing. Most children move exactly like that when they speak in front of the class. They sway from side to side and suddenly don't seem to have a clue what they actually wanted to say.

No filter – Filters develop slowly. As a baby, there is no need for one. If you are unhappy, you cry. If you are amused, you laugh. If you don't like the food, you spit it out. By elementary school age most kids have begun to develop some filter, but it is faulty. This results in sometimes refreshing, but oftentimes brutal honesty. Don't be offended when a kindergarten kid asks you why your skin is so loose on your elbows. But on the flip side, don't be overly flattered when that same kid tells you that you are the best or most beautiful teacher he has ever had. Compared to whom?

Tantrums – Where do I begin? Tantrums run a whole range of intensities. There is the classic style whole-body flung onto the floor, legs kicking and arms flailing. This method seems so ridiculous to me that I often have to stifle my urge to laugh. Some kids choose the arms crossed on the chest accompanied by a scowl. This quiet protest is easily ignored. Refusal in the form of a tantrum has never had the intended outcome in my classroom. I can ignore and outlast even the most determined performance. It is most effective if you can bring yourself to just calmly step over the prone and fist-pounding tyrant and carry on teaching. Without the desired reaction an encore rarely occurs.

Tappers – Perhaps the most annoying of all attention-seeking children, the tappers generally move into position when you are busy helping another child. They start out gently enough, poking or patting your arm or leg quietly and rhythmically. If you tune them out, which I am a master at, they gradually increase the tempo and intensity of the poking until you are suddenly painfully aware that you are being pummelled and you whirl around to face the aggressor. Startled by the very attention they were just seeking, the flustered child usually forgets what they wanted in the first place.

Concentration (or lack thereof) – A recent photo taken of my firefighter son and his Dalmatian dog surrounded by kindergarteners at a fire safety course is a perfect snapshot of childhood concentration in action. Despite calling everybody's attention to the photographer, at the moment this photo was snapped exactly one child out of the twenty kids present is actually looking at the camera. He is smiling confidently and proudly holding his participation certificate at his chest with his plastic firefighter hat squarely on his head.

A scan of the other kids in the photo reveals less than perfect posing. One youngster is pulling at the chinstrap of his fire hat as if he were being strangled. Three grinning and delighted little monkeys know that a group photo is not complete without bunny ears. One is resting his chin on Mr. Firefighter's head while making bunny ears, the second is making bunny ears on the dog, and the third vertically challenged kiddo is attempting to make his bunny ears on Mr. Firefighter's shoulder.

Questionable brain function flickers on the face of one vacant cherub who appears to be in a trance. Another poor little bugger looks like his pet turtle just died. The kid closest to the dog is gazing at his new canine best friend with pure love and adoration.

The thing is, when I scrolled through the half dozen photos taken in quick succession in this twenty-second photo shoot, this is the photo I nailed as a good one, a real keeper.

Fast-forward twelve years to a hypothetical class photo of the same kids at high school graduation and (knowing how personality works) I can predict the results. Described in the same order as the above: The class valedictorian holds his diploma at his chest. His robe is done up properly, bedecked in cords and sashes recognizing all of his achievements and his graduation cap sits squarely on his head as he smiles confidently at the camera.

Chinstrap boy is not wearing his graduation cap because it annoys him. The bunny ears gang are all smiling with pride and genuine joy as they do bunny ears at the back of each other's heads; robes undone to show their superhero T-shirts, torn jeans and athletic shoes underneath.

Vacant kid still looks vacant and the trance is now a record breaking twelve years on. Dead turtle boy has a tattoo of his turtle on his shoulder, which we can see because he has removed the sleeves of his robe for that purpose. The Dalmatian admirer remembers the fire safety day like it was yesterday, owns a Dalmatian of his own, plans to be a firefighter and has replaced his graduation cap with the plastic firefighter hat he has saved for twelve years and it doesn't fit all that swell.

Helpful Hannahs – It seems like having a Helpful Hannah in your class would be a blessing, right? Well… that depends. Sometimes these kids can be enormously useful, but it all depends on the approach. Like the clothing store clerk that shadows you and suggests items you surely must need, pushes relentlessly and tells you that everything looks absolutely smashing on you, these little personal assistants can often drive you insane while desperately trying to make your life easier.

They sense your rising stress levels like a well-trained assistance dog and swoop to the rescue even if it derails your lesson altogether because they have misread your next move. At even the slightest mention of a possible written task the helpful one will jump up and force a whiteboard marker into your hand, then rush over and start unloading whichever exercise book she deems appropriate for the task at hand. This frenzied activity may be accompanied by shouting, "It's OK! I got this, Mrs. Davis!"

I did have a future Secretary of the Year in my fourth grade class one year who took it upon herself to straighten my desk, my office and sometimes even my school bag with efficient regularity. She was actually extremely helpful. I am not sure how much she learned that year, but I learned some very valuable organisational techniques. Mainly her strategies were in the chuck-it-in-the-bin category of filing, but it was so cleansing. As a general rule, the younger the Helpful Hannah the more likely she is to truly want to help, but the less likely it is that the help delivered will actually save you any time or effort.

I realise that I have only addressed a handful of behaviours here, but this is not meant to be a behaviour analysis book. My mother's theory (having successfully raised six of us) is this. She believes that as a parent you have a lot of influence over a child's ultimate behaviour, but the underlying personality is there from birth. Therefore, we can influence and guide towards appropriate behaviour, but you will not change the personality driving that behaviour. Her theory has guided me through raising my four kids and teaching thousands of students over the years. Celebrate the diversity! If we are prepared to accept the nature of the beast that is the tiny human, we will cope with the behaviours.

So basically the point I am trying to make here is that (regardless of the age or grade level) human nature is not going to be predictable. Very few real children are going to behave in a way that fits nicely into the scenarios discussed in your university behaviour management class or the most recent seminar you attended. Let common sense, caring and compassion be your guide.

Further on in this book I address annoying habits and so-called naughty behaviour. Unacceptable behaviours sometimes have deep rooted causes. Don't let anybody talk you into any one-size-fits-all behaviour management plans. All that you can really effectively manage is your own reaction.

Unsolicited advice:

1. Forget any preconceived notions you may have about personal body space.
2. Get to truly know each kid.
3. Just deal with it.

Setting and Supplies

According to some experts, proper classroom design is essential for academic success. Adequate school supplies are also helpful. However, while delving into these requirements in more depth, we must bear in mind that all over the world some pretty fantastic learning with the support of dedicated teachers is happening in mud huts, open air classrooms with dirt floors and old shipping containers.

Buying into the theory of the importance of a well-designed classroom environment, we are back to the question of just what is a proper classroom design? Back in my substitute teaching days I saw rooms that ran the full gamut of learning environments. Some were quite pleasant and some most definitely were not. Seeing this range of environments before setting up a classroom of my own helped me form clear ideas of what I did and didn't want mine to look like.

I saw military-style rooms with neat rows of desks equidistant from each other and all books, maps, supplies, etc. carefully organised in categories and labelled. My German teacher in high school had such a room. Not only did he rearrange desks (with people in them) if they scooted a little out of line with the row, but he actually adjusted people within the seats if they were not centred as well.

One year two mischievous boys, who happened to be twins, were enrolled in my German class. Not only did they try to play havoc with this poor OCD educator by impersonating each other, but they also liked to tamper with the belongings on his desk. One fine day before Herr OCD arrived these brothers carefully removed one of the bookends from the row of books he kept neatly lined up in graduating height along the front edge of his desk.

Inevitably at some point during that day's riveting lecture the first book fell. The others followed like dominos, crashing onto the floor waking several students who were doing an admirable job of sleeping with their eyes open.

This incident is most memorable for the reaction of Herr OCD. He didn't even blink. He continued to lecture as he carefully picked up and arranged the books back in the exact order they had been in before being tampered with. Then he strolled slowly and deliberately past the twins and snapped his fingers, at which one of them produced the bookend and he strolled back up and placed it against the end of the book row. All the while he conducted class. Now that, my friend, is order.

At the other end of the spectrum we have classrooms that look for-all-the-world like the aftermath of an F-5 tornado. I encountered an alarming number of classrooms in this category during my substitute teaching days.

A science teacher I filled in for more than once was a master at disguising his desk. If you were not in a classroom and specifically looking for a desk, you would never have known there was one in there. A paper haystack of impressive girth and height adorned his desk. The student desks were helter-skelter about the room with papers and pencils from yesterday's work strewn about on the crayon marked surfaces.

As I sat down at the haystack to look for the obligatory note to the substitute teacher I heard a rustling in the shelves behind me. Twirling around to look, I thought I saw a ripple run through the debris on the shelves. Nervously turning back to shovel through the haystack some more I spotted a newer looking, unwrinkled sheet of paper that held promise as my note. Sure enough, there was a brief message with some vague instructions. The note finished with, "P.S. If you find my rat, please put him back in the cage."

OK. So, the rustling was real. Swivelling slowly back around, I found myself face to face with a red-eyed, rather hungry looking white lab rat. Lucky for me, I am by nature a calm person and not particularly afraid of furry creatures. Catching this particular rat proved to be an interesting and sweat inducing exercise, but once he was captured I had a new problem. Where was the cage…?

Back in my own school days in the 60s and 70s, classroom décor was subject to the hand and whim of the resident teacher. If she liked flowers, you had flowers. If she liked Disney characters, you had Disney characters.

From my own childhood, I particularly remember two rooms. One was my kindergarten room. This room had a huge wall of windows overlooking a lake and a large colourful rug in the middle of the linoleum floor where we gathered to be enlightened by a teacher that I can no longer put a name or face to. To my unending delight it also had little tables and chairs that were just the right size for me. I am a tall drink of water now, but back in the day I was one of the little ones and those tiny chairs were, in my opinion, the best things going in that room.

I don't remember even one word that that woman said to us, but I do remember the little chairs where my feet actually touched the ground. I couldn't wait for her to stop talking so I could go claim a chair at one of those miniature tables to do whatever task we had been assigned. I also remember that there were colourful alphabet cards along the top of the wall near the ceiling and each one had a picture to go with it: Aa with an apple, Bb with a boat, etc. I am sure that my teacher had put great time and effort into that room. There may have even been flowers or Disney characters, but for me the big windows, tiny chairs and intriguing alphabet cards did the trick.

The other room that I distinctly remember was where I had my high school history class. This room had walls plastered with wordless posters of people from all nations and walks of life. When my mind wandered, which it did frequently, I could stare at those posters and think about all the different lives being led all around the world.

Chairs with the little half desk attached were arranged in a circle to facilitate discussion – a radical idea in the early 70s. Our scruffy, longhaired teacher would float about the room in his bellbottom pants, perching on the edge of a desk here or there to stroke his stubbly beard and muse on historical and political beliefs. I remember that the discussions were deep and often confusing, but it was the configuration of the room forcing us to face one another and the faces of all those people on the posters that made me think deeply about human behaviour and its global consequences.

Ever since becoming a full-time teacher in the USA the freedom to create a learning environment with my own flair seemed to rapidly erode. The amount of leeway I had in decorating my classrooms over the years varied depending on the school and the school administration. But, each year it seemed that the reigns got decidedly tighter.

At one point in my career some new research concerning classroom design revealed a great flaw in the time-honoured tradition of blasting young senses with stimuli. Once these new findings about the dangers of overstimulation were brought to the attention of our school administration the school makeover began. This included changing the colours in every classroom from the traditional bright primary and secondary colours to calmer colours chosen from a specific colour pallet carefully selected to avoid the dreaded overstimulation

Apparently colour was now distracting. To minimize all this distraction we were also directed to take down any silly pictures or colourful, decorative flim-flam, which could potentially detract from the soothing walls newly painted in the approved colours of cream, pea soup and grey. All of our cute bulletin board borders with little children holding hands, or multicoloured stars, or cartoon animals had to go in favour of black. We were provided with black border for our convenience. It actually ended up looking pretty sharp – if the school were a business office!

I returned home from our little in-service on dulling down and promptly rang up all of my grown children to apologise for any damage I may have done to their intellectual development by hanging multi coloured alphabet curtains, wild paintings and Disney characters on the walls. They also had been subjected to sheets and blankets busy with dinosaurs, princesses and more Disney characters, and I had topped it all off with multi-hued mobiles dangling above their cribs. It was clear that falling a bit short of perfect scores on college entrance exams was most assuredly my fault entirely. If only I had known of the danger of overstimulation back then.

Modern classroom décor in Colorado also took a substantial hit from the Fire Marshal. No more paper lanterns or pumpkins hanging from the ceiling. No more finger paintings or construction paper artwork on the walls. We were directed to keep the percentage of each wall covered by paper to less than 20%.

During the four years that I was on first grade we taught a unit on animal and plant adaptation. As part of this unit each year we built a glorious floor to ceiling paper kapok tree in the classroom, complete with buttressing roots and a canopy that spread out across a sizable portion of the ceiling. We loaded our mini-rainforest up with paper plants and animals.

Without a shadow of a doubt, this kapok tree was an enormous fire torch and in direct violation of every section of the school fire code. This magnificent creation really stood out once there was no other colour in the room. Mercifully our principal judiciously avoided entering our first grade classrooms during this unit, so as to avoid having to notice this flagrant code violation.

I am back in Australia now and thankfully the fire fighters here have better things to do than check what percentage of a classroom wall might be covered by paper. My first year back I happily dangled watercolour masterpieces and impressive works of mathematical genius on fishing line strung from the rafters. Additional displays of nine-year-old student brilliance adorned the brick walls. The room actually looked like a space occupied by kids!

Unfortunately there is not a lot that can be done about the physical structure of buildings and classrooms. The best rooms I have taught in have been those built before the 70s. These rooms have walls and windows. Walls are nice. Windows are nice.

Let me explain. About the same time that students were expected to work collaboratively on nearly everything the concept of a wall became bad. Open plan schools proliferated. Even as a generation of teachers began to lose their voices and eventually their minds, architects clamoured to outdo each other creating schools that could win awards rather than designing spaces where a person might hear themselves think for a few seconds each day.

A round two-story school in my hometown in Minnesota was built during this era with all of the rooms on both floors open to a central library. By open I mean that one entire side of each classroom faced the library and had no wall. The piece-of-pie shaped rooms 'flowed' into the round hallway, which was a balcony overlooking the library on the second floor and the library itself on the ground floor. The library became a giant echo chamber.

Teachers went two ways in their attempts to cope with the chaos. Some went stealth mode with their kids trying to respect the inherent right of others to avoid hearing aids until at least the ripe old age of thirty. Others decided that the best course of action was to just be louder than the class next door or across the labyrinth (I mean library) from them. I only taught for a one-term contract at this school but feel that I retain some latent crowd avoidance issues as a result.

The middle school in Colorado (grades 6-8) where I taught science for a year was genuinely an architectural award winning design – meaning it had won an actual award. From the outside it had the appearance of an art gallery turned prison or perhaps the other way around. Smatterings of oddly sized and geometrically shaped windows were randomly arranged on the walls so there appeared to be no distinct floor levels when viewed from the outside. The result on the inside was that a room might end up with two small square windows about the size of your head up near the ceiling or a long skinny rectangular window at the floor. None of the windows opened, there was very little natural light and there were no real views from any classroom despite a spectacular hilltop site overlooking the front range of the Rocky Mountains. Perhaps the architects didn't completely understand the purposes of windows.

This school had also been constructed from steel and concrete that would surely endure a nuclear blast. This meant that mobile phones did not function well. Imagine a building full of adolescents deprived of constant communication with everybody they know in their media saturated little universe. Couple that with a lack of opportunity to even create a hand signalling system due to a lack of any windows at head height and you have a recipe for frustration and discontent.

Luckily for the kids (and teachers) another artsy feature of this school was the bevy of exposed metal beams. In our science teacher's office there was a convenient beam running from floor to ceiling along one wall at a 45-degree angle. We were all as nimble as monkeys by the end of the year as a result of our daily scampering up the beam to crouch near the ceiling where we could get cell phone reception.

Significant consideration is given to the subject of seating arrangements in some teacher guidebooks, often complete with diagrams and everything. Now these are fun to look at if you have absolutely nothing else to do with your life. However, all the feng shui in the world is not going to help when the hummers, tappers, snifflers or just plain old aggravating little people are paired with somebody with a low tolerance for distraction.

I have tried just about every configuration that a teacher can dream up for thirty little desks or a bunch of tables and there is no such a thing as the perfect set up. I attended primary school in the early 60s when the standard configuration was simply straight rows of desks. This worked OK then because we had those desks with the attached seats and the tops that you lifted up to get at the stuff inside.

I remember the ritual at the beginning of each new school year when the custodian would clump in with a big wrench and adjust the seat and desktop to each child's height. As I said earlier, I am tall now, but I was one of the smallest back then and if a tall kid sat behind me his desk top actually lined up nicely with the back of my head. This meant no drifting off or I would crack the back of my head. If the tall guy was in front me – with his height-adjusted seat – there was no hope of seeing the board, and everything happened on the board back then. The other fun thing about those lift top desks was that when kids tried to lift the lid just enough to sneak something out without taking everything off the top it sent their books and pencils cascading onto the back of the person in front of them. Good times.

Rows are frowned upon in these days of cooperative learning. They wouldn't work anyway because with a freestanding desk and a little plastic chair, lining them up in rows only sets you up for crushing injuries. When Tubby Todd stands up he invariably pushes himself up off the front of his desk. This propels it forward into Skinny Minnie's plastic chair, which follows all the laws of motion and scoots forward smashing Skinny Minnie's ribs into the front edge of her own desk. Aside from the internal injury hazard, rows are also out because kids these days are supposed to be collaborating on their work and that is best done in some sort of partnership or group.

When I taught first grade in Colorado I used foursomes. Two kids sat side by side. This next-door neighbour became their 'elbow partner'. This pair of desks was pushed face to face with two other desks with slight adjustments for uneven numbers. This was conducive to cooperative work, kept the desks in relatively the right positions and had the added benefit of being ideal for getting off task with ease.

The tappers, jigglers and hummers carried on with what they did best, while the easily aggravated elbow partner built up internal pressure until she snatched the offending pencil, hip checked the jiggling one or finally yelled *stop* in that pitch and tone only achievable when your voice is still several octaves higher than humanly possible for an adult. In the end the best thing to do is to just change the whole thing up often enough that no child builds up such an enduring grudge that they stalk and murder their elbow partner later in life.

In classrooms where there are tables rather than desks (with supplies kept in tote trays) the whole arrangement can be much more flexible. Every now and again you can let the kids choose who they want to sit with. You can end up with some really effective little working groups for a while. Unfortunately most kids are not super duper effective learners while giggling with their best friends and inevitably most of them make some very bad choices.

Think about staff meetings. When we sit with our best friends we can often have difficulty with focus and attention too. Something about the presentation strikes your funny bone. You simply lean over and whisper your amusing off-topic comment in the ear of your buddy. Your pal gets the giggles and the rest of the meeting becomes an enormous struggle to maintain composure. You and your friend find it highly amusing, but nobody else is in on the joke and finds you incredibly annoying and immature. However, regardless of the fact that most of us have strayed from the path on occasion, we still find this a very serious offense when committed by a child.

In addition to the arrangement of desks, wall decoration, paint colour, etc. there is consideration to be given to the supplies available in your room. I will attack this from a kindergarten perspective since that is the most fun. As far as I am concerned there are certain items that do not belong in a primary level classroom at all – ever.

I will begin with Super Glue. If visions of permanently glued fingertips, hair attached to desks and lunch boxes permanently joined to the floor are not enough imagery for you then I can't help. No super glue – ever – period.

Next on my list are permanent markers. Whiteboards, brick walls and classmates' faces do not fare well when marred by this ink. I do keep a few of these around for labelling things, but they are buried in my desk drawer for safekeeping, preferably beneath a few off-putting items like crumpled tissues or thumbtacks.

Liquid glue is also kept where little hands do not have ready access – for obvious reasons. Glue sticks work just fine. I do feel a bit bad that I am depriving my class of the satisfying sensory experience of applying a thin smearing of glue to their skin, letting it dry and then slowly peeling it off. The pleasure here is mostly in the peeling sensation on the skin, but the secondary benefit if the film comes off in one piece is a forensic quality fingerprint. The crème de la crème of glue peeling. However my students have plenty of other distractions to keep them occupied, so the liquid glue stays tucked away.

Clay and play dough also need to be contained and only brought forth when a supervised activity is underway. These substances have all sorts of valid educational purposes ranging from creativity, to sensory stimulation, to 3D representation of all sorts of concepts. The downfall here is the insidious way that this material works its way into carpets, hair and sink drains. It also falls (with broad interpretation) into the edible items category.

I do allow my students to have scissors. There are two reasons for this. One is that no modern school supply company with any shred of self-preservation makes a child's scissors that can actually pierce anything without a substantial run-up, much less easily cut anything – except human hair. Try as you might you are unlikely to get these super-safe scissors to cleanly cut paper, but when cutting a classmate's hair that chunk just snips right out with ease. It is as if the cheap little plastic device has suddenly developed laser sharp qualities. The other perfectly valid reason for allowing personal possession of scissors is obvious to me. How can I possibly utter that iconic teacher command of, "No running with scissors!" if nobody has scissors?

In a whole different category of banned goods, totally unrelated to mayhem and destruction, are things like character Band-Aids. Of course the whole point in marketing character Band-Aids is to sell more of them. One of my former schools bought a batch of these fun Band-Aids with cartoon characters and animals on them and they were used up school wide within one day. I don't think kids were actually purposely self-inflicting wounds, but coincidentally there was a rash of injury that day. Paper cuts, picked scabs and miniscule scrapes needing drastic and immediate bandaging occurred with unprecedented frequency all day. When resupplied with standard pink Band-Aids the next day, the need immediately dropped off again.

Pop-up books are a total waste of money in a primary classroom or in the hands of anybody young enough to get a thrill from them. Nobody ever purposely rips up these books. They simply self-destruct. I'm sure the makers of these stimulating books envision hours of fascination and delight from their 3D masterpieces, but they seldom last past the first viewing. It is not because all kids are destructive by nature (which is a perfectly valid and provable theory), it is more about the complexity of the books themselves. Me being one of those people that can never *ever* refold a paper road map correctly once it is opened all the way up, I totally comprehend the enormous challenge presented by turning the page of a pop-up book. If you open it just a teeny tiny bit too far your chances of going on to the next page cleanly are next to none.

To replace outdated or inconvenient educational supplies we now have smart boards, document cameras, computers, iPads and other nifty devices. Incredible as these technological devices are they come with another set of management issues. We can firewall to the hilt, but each new generation of students is born with additional genes that enable them to circumvent any and all blocking techniques we may employ.

I learned to *not* blindly believe in the effectiveness of these security measures early on in the computer availability age. When I was teaching fourth grade in an American school I was helping students edit writing when the class snitch came over to inform me that a classmate was looking at 'hot girls' on the computer. The trustworthy young man in question had been allowed on a computer to finish researching a paper he was writing, which as far as I knew had nothing to do with saunas, tropical beaches or hard workouts. At that moment I was busy and knew that firewalls were in place if my student was in fact searching a different kind of 'hot girl'.

So, I waved off the fine upstanding citizen (who was undoubtedly concerned only with preserving her classmate's moral character) with a lame assertion that the school had measures in place to prevent students from viewing anything inappropriate. Moments later the little tattletale was back insisting that this juvenile perv was still looking at hot girls.

Exasperated, I turned to her and asked her to just whisper in my ear what she had seen on the screen. As soon as she painted a mental image for me I leaped up, scattering unedited papers and junior authors in my wake, as I dashed over to shut down his screen. Seeing me lunging towards him, he beat me to it and had clicked out of the offending site before I got there. Lucky for me, and unfortunate for him, our school tech guy was able to login and trace this ten-year-old knowledge seeker's recent online history. He had numerous searches in the hot girls and related categories. This resulted in a computer ban for him and a lesson learnt for all involved.

Despite awesome new technology, good old traditional office supplies still hold an esteemed place in the hearts of most teachers. Recently our principal arrived in our unit with a giant box of office supplies scrounged from around the school after we whined about our lack of pencils, etc. As Santa clomped in bearing these revered gifts we teachers were in near rhapsody over the sight of a box full of pencils, kids' scissors, a whole unopened box of staples, two brand new staplers to put them in, a dozen glue sticks, several exercise books, half a dozen pads of post-it notes, a clump of erasers, two student dictionaries, some brand new whiteboard markers and a couple of 70s era calculators. Score! We were stoked!

My first year on kindergarten I was excited to be tackling the last piece of the puzzle that is my diverse career. I came in several days in advance of the official teacher start days to set up my classroom. Being a bit of a minimalist, the resulting learning space was not likely to end up adorning the cover of a teacher magazine, but I was pretty proud of my efforts. The kids, being new to formal schooling, were delighted to have their own desk space, tote tray, book bag, etc. Things were going well... until the flood.

One dark and stormy night it rained so hard and for so long that a torrent of muddy water poured under the door of our kindergarten building and converted my lovely classroom into a swamp. Yes – just my classroom, which was apparently lower than the other two. Having grown up in Minnesota where flooded basements are a springtime ritual, I knew we were not going to be occupying that soggy and decidedly stinky space anytime in the immediate future.

The experts engaged by the school to assess the damage thought differently. They doggedly tried to dry the carpets with giant fans. When that failed they washed and then dried them again. The stench endured. By the end of the second week they were pulling up all the carpet tiles, washing them yet again and then drying them in the hot sun.

Meanwhile, my twenty-eight students and I set up camp in the school library. This turned out to be quite a lovely quiet retreat for us. We enjoyed our little sanctuary for about a week, before the other two kindergarten classes bailed out of the rapidly deteriorating conditions in the flood zone and joined us. We now had eighty-one kindergarteners, three teachers and a frazzled and beleaguered librarian sharing the limited spaces amongst the book stacks. We were there for about three weeks. Teaching in a labyrinth. Good times.

For weeks and months after our return to our own classroom, the students reminisced about the 'old days' whenever we visited the library. Pointing to their artworks, which remained on the walls, they would sigh and say things like, "Remember when we could just get a new book anytime we wanted?" School is really about the moments, not the perfect classroom design.

My advice on classroom design:

1. Don't overthink it.
2. Consider blinders (like racehorses wear) for every child.
3. Don't get too attached to your room.

All of the Students - All of the Time

Every child can learn. The research assures us that all we need to do is simply 'engage all of the students all of the time'. We all believe this to our very core of course. Truly we do.

It wasn't always this way. Even just a few years ago there was a streak of realism in all of us that allowed us to be OK with getting some of our less gifted little charges just a tad further down the road with as little emotional damage as possible.

We are now expected to ensure that all kids make a 'full year's growth' each school year. Never mind that a child who is two years behind his peers by fourth grade quite obviously *grows* at a different rate. We are told to differentiate, but that apparently does not include differentiating the expected rate of learning despite all the evidence in a particular child's educational history pointing to the fact that the child takes more time to get there. Having been a PE teacher I can assure you that even with all the intervention in the world every child will not run a mile at the same pace, so I have a hard time understanding why we expect every child to learn at the same rate.

We must remember that the adults whom we encounter in our daily interactions within our community were once children in school. For instance you might encounter a cheerful, yet decidedly slow checkout clerk. This adult most likely attended school and despite a whole series of teachers over the course of thirteen years still can't make change for a dollar. The odds of every single one of those thirteen teachers being sub-par are astronomical. Surely the less than perfect results of an individual's education have at least a little bit to do with genetic material. I wholeheartedly agree that all children can learn. I am just suggesting that maybe not all children learn everything at the same rate (and to the same level of understanding) in every academic area.

I can't spell well. Nor can I read fast. Despite these appalling shortcomings, I have successfully completed two Bachelor's degrees, a Master's degree and numerous non-university qualifications. Spell check, combined with patient friends and relatives allowed me to come to grips with my spelling handicap. However, speed-reading will never be in my bag of tricks. I once took a speed-reading course at university that touted guaranteed results. I failed. Entirely coincidentally, the frustrated instructor retired that same year.

Current thinking in the field of education tells us that the teacher is the deciding factor in student success. While I completely agree with this in theory, I really feel that it is highly unlikely that even the best teacher in the whole universe is going to reach every child, every time and all of the time. All we can do is set up our educational environment in such a way that we can reach as many kids as possible in that particular place and time.

It's fascinating to me that the new buzzword in education is *inquiry*. I extend my apologies to those who object to me calling it a buzzword. I wholeheartedly believe in inquiry-based learning. Most scientific discoveries of any real significance, and possibly our entire collective human knowledge from the dawn of mankind, are the result of human inquiry.

As a student of the 60s and early 70s my personal experience with formal schooling was mostly in the realm of taught knowledge. The teacher talked and we listened. The teacher wrote stuff on the chalkboard and we copied. This factory style approach to education only developed with the widespread acceptance of mass formal schooling just a couple of generations before mine. Before that, the great scholars and inventors that brought us many of the innovations that allow our current lifestyle were natural inquirers. Children are natural inquirers. Inquiry learning is not new!

I acknowledge the need to somehow structure the vast scope of human knowledge we now require to navigate our modern world. The proliferation of common outcomes and standards at school, local, state, national and international levels is testament to the value now placed on providing a comprehensive education for all citizens. Many nations have developed a set of educational standards to meet the needs of their people, while still attempting to include a global outlook. Never mind that there is very little chance that Jonah, who wishes to one day inherit his father's fishing boat, is not all that interested in balancing chemical equations or solving trigonometry problems. Whereas, the future Dr. Bones IV is likewise unimpressed with learning the possible causes of the dismal plight of the tuna fish populations worldwide.

Yet despite varied interests and passions, as we seek to return to inquiry as one of the most basic of human instincts, we still feel the need to structure the 'activity' of inquiry. We tell the kids, "Now we are going to inquire into *the changes in exploration today through technological advances."* To the modern day teacher this seems very open-ended and allows ample room to explore and inquire, but to the kid who is not even remotely interested in technological advances this is still restrictive. I am not convinced we can call it true inquiry if we narrow the focus too much. Inquiry is not a subject!

One year after visiting the student science fair at our school, my colleague and I invited our two classes of year four students (nine and ten-year-olds) to ask questions about 'absolutely anything' they were wondering about. We asked them to write their questions on bits of coloured paper and post them on a large bulletin board for everyone to ponder and/or investigate.

It took us nearly twenty minutes to get them to understand that there was no right or wrong genre of question they could ask. These questions were not restricted to the science fair they had just attended, or any specific subject, or the earth, the universe, or even anything tangible at all. Some of the children still focused mainly on the science projects they had just seen, but the vast majority took flight with their imaginations. They filled the board.

The following sample of *actual questions* were the delightful result:

Why don't fish have eyebrows? What would happen if you reversed the rotation of the earth? Why is one flower red and another might be yellow? Is there such a thing as aliens? Why do wet tongues stick to cold metal poles? Why is our body made of water? Is there life in other universes? How and why does gravity work? Why are there planets? Will the earth ever end? When and how? Why am I myself and not somebody else? What happens if friction doesn't counteract force? What causes force? How and when did life come to our planet and why? When was the first person? Why is metal attracted to a magnet? Is time always the same? Why are all the planets different sizes? How did the dinosaurs come alive? How was gravity created? What makes us love? Why do people need hair? Why do people have feelings? Is there other life in the universe?

How were all the planets created? How did the big bang do the big bang at that specific time? Why are humans so special compared to animals? Why do people get old? How was the first germ created? If we had another life, what would it be? When was the first living form and what was it? Why are humans creative? What is on the other side of a black hole? Why does time exist? Why is the universe infinite? If the universe is not infinite, what is on the other side of the end? And my favourite: Is there actually a present? Because the question I just asked is already in the past and the next word I am about to say is still in the future.

Wow! Now that is inquiry!

Getting back to this intent to **engage all of the students, all of the time**. In my opinion this is just a mythical scenario dreamed up by educational research people who have the time and grant money to dream such lofty dreams. Believing that all students will be engaged in every lesson you teach is like a chef believing that every patron that enters his restaurant will love his chef's special.

Now don't get me wrong, we have all had those beautiful moments in the sun; those glorious snippets of time when you have the whole class in the palm of your hand. These moments usually involve making a fool of yourself in some manner or other. When the kids are in hysterics they are usually with you.

All you have to do with six-year olds is pretend you don't notice a mistake or ask them to please don't do something you know they want to do. For example if you are trying out different letters or letter blends and asking students to respond on their whiteboards and you are using *it* as your ending, you can let them try a few words such as; fit, sit, bit, slit, then say, "But be careful. Don't you dare go putting a *sh* in front of your *it*." As soon as they realise what word it makes they are in giggles and get busy trying to think of other combinations that are not allowed. They are fully engaged in phonics. This is easy to do with first graders. Eighth grade science students are a harder crowd.

When I taught eighth grade chemistry and physics, the moments when I was certain, without a shadow of a doubt, that I had my adolescent miscreants in the palm of my hand were those times when I had failed miserably with a scientific demonstration. This was especially true if it involved a spectacular display of chemicals, fire, or a substance altering its state in an unpredicted or undesirable manner. There is nothing quite as sweet when you are thirteen years old than your teacher falling flat on her face.

To my surprise and satisfaction however, these same pseudo-adults were equally thrilled to simply watch dry ice dance across the lab demo table. I don't even remember what we were using the dry ice for one particular day, but we all learned to our collective delight, that dry ice will literally jump and travel about when placed on a science lab tabletop. I am not convinced there is any practical real-world application for that particular knowledge of dry ice behaviour, but I do know that the moment I spilled a scoopful of dry ice chunks on that counter top, true student engagement had been accomplished.

Similarly, I had full participation in my class one year in Australia when I managed to capture a yippy, snappy little dog that scampered into the classroom as the kids were entering via the outside door one morning. Getting inside the classroom had been a long-term goal of this crazy canine since the first day of school when he accompanied his best friend to school. This fine morning the deranged doggy had either drunk a gallon or so of coffee or had some sort of doggy mania, because he tore around the room jumping at kids and barking.

This was a new dilemma for me and since the parent who owned the dog had no more control over Fido than her kid, it was up to me to remove this shaggy learning distraction. In the end I actually ended up snagging Fido's collar pretty much by accident as he made his eighty-seventh pass around the back of the reading corner.

I reached down as he zipped past and (uncharacteristically for me) made a smooth catch with three fingers under his collar. "You, my friend, are not following the rules," I quipped as I unceremoniously deposited the crazy canine outside. All eyes were on me. No need for any bell work, anticipatory set, or other attention getters that morning! I had no cape, but I was a hero for pretty much the rest of that whole day.

So, aside from unusual circumstances and rare adrenaline producing occurrences, how do we get and hold attention and then manage to impart some sort of knowledge or guide student inquiry so that our students learn something every day? Current educational lingo calls it TPTs for Total Participation Techniques.

Back in my day the teachers didn't much care if we were paying attention or not, as long as we were quiet. These days a quiet kid is a non-participating kid and that is not OK. If a student is not responding on a whiteboard or putting their hand up incessantly, they are surely not learning. Who learns by listening anymore, anyhow? Seriously.

So, the trick is to make the lesson introduction intriguing enough to draw the students in. Then your delivery of the lesson needs to be either hands-on or practically a Broadway worthy performance in order to be sure everybody is engaged at all times. Next the students eagerly apply the new knowledge or skill independently or in small groups. Also, you must have a viable plan for assessing whether or not they have actually learned whatever it is that you wanted them to learn. If you do all of this, while still being sensitive to all possible cultural, emotional, and social differences you are golden. Simple really.

Take telling time for instance. One of the first grade standards when I taught in Colorado stated that,

'Students will be able to tell and write time in hours and half hours using analogue and digital clocks'. This was a challenging skill even back when I was a kid, but now it is really rough, because the only analog clock (which is the round one with the hands by the way) that they ever see is the one in the classroom. They understand the digital version pretty quickly, but it doesn't matter how many times you pass out the little wooden practice clocks (that were surely made by Gepetto himself) and have the kids push the little hands around into position, they will still get it wrong as soon as you are not guiding them. Did you know that if the little hand is on the three and the big hand is on the seven, the time is 3:7 and if the little hand is on the five and the big hand is on the twelve the time is 5:12? Some students will even say five o'clock and write it 5:12 or 12:5. I judiciously stockpiled enough staff leave days that I could get a sub for all those days when clocks were in the lesson plans.

A colleague related to me a perfect example of the divergent levels of thought students can have when presented with a hypothetical question. When a group of her fifth grade students were asked if the world would be different today if Sir Isaac Newton had not discovered gravity most of the students were pretty sure things would be quite drastically different. Only a small group argued that most likely things would be the same, because somebody else surely would have discovered it by now anyhow and even if nobody had noticed it, gravity would still be doing its thing. But one poor kid (destined to hold a road construction sign as a career choice) was adamant that if Sir Isaac had not noticed and named this phenomenon we most assuredly would all be 'floating around out in space'.

Those students who fall far enough out of the norm get placed on individual learning plans. These have names like ILP (Individual Learning Plan) and IEP (Individual Education Plan). Despite the lack of formal plans, the majority of effective teachers have always made adjustments and accommodations for kids who don't access the regular curriculum in the same manner as the typical student.

In some cases the writing up of a formal plan may ensure that the child receives the attention he or she needs. However, I maintain that for all of us who already spend time creating meaningful learning experiences for every child the paperwork generated by these plans has served to cut into the time we have for carrying out our plans and creating more. Well-intentioned legislation often causes unintended consequences.

Despite adding more science and technology subjects each year we still stubbornly hang onto all the old things too and try to cram it all into the same school hours. Even though our curriculum is overloaded and all children must learn the same standards we still are required to differentiate how they learn those standards.

This means we must figure out whether little Susie learns best by standing on her head or whether she prefers soft music and a balance ball to function at her optimal level. Once we figure out her optimal setting, mode of delivery, level of support and preferred learning style we must then make sure that not only are her particular needs being met, but also that the needs of the twenty plus other children in the room are being precisely catered to as well. This, my friend, is called differentiation.

All kids learn differently, so differentiation is educational jargon for making sure we take all the different learning styles into consideration. Who is going to argue with that in theory? The reality of that directive is quite another story altogether.

Reaching back to our teacher training in the multiple intelligences we can attempt to reach each child through his or her best learning style. Let's take a lesson on exclamation points as a working example of the complications that can arise when we try to teach this lesson to a diverse group of learners.

Little Annie Academic will sit still and watch you write this new punctuation mark on the board, copy it on her whiteboard, and then seamlessly work it into her writing in all the appropriate places. She is a verbal-linguistic genius and this new way to express herself on paper has just opened whole new worlds of possibility. She is stoked.

However, active Johnny Jumper is a bodily-kinaesthetic learner and will need you to demo the action part of this confusing new symbol in order for him to take it on board. You will jump up (at risk of life and limb) clapping your hands together above your head and land nimble-footed and balanced precariously on a soccer ball in perfect imitation of this exciting new punctuation mark. He and his fellow bodily-kinaesthetic learners will need to repeat this with you approximately forty-seven times in quick succession in order to cement it into their long-term memories. As you reach total exhaustion, you realise this has been mucho-funno, but there are all those other multiple intelligences out there still to be addressed.

Meanwhile over in another learning realm altogether, little flighty Sunbeam Feather Sunrise and her fellow would-be hippy throwbacks that learn in the land of the visual-spatial are busy altering your drawing of an exclamation point to include a heart for the dot and the top part filled with rainbow colours. This is all good. Let it go.

Tiring of the calisthenics, the intrapersonal learners are wanting to know how all of this relates to their inner-selves and will need some intensive counselling later in life if you don't get down off the soccer ball and figure out a way to make a connection to their inner being.

Inspired by distant memories flickering through your brain from that course you took on the multiple intelligences back in the early 80s you quickly gather all the kids, take them outside and find sticks that will help the nature-smart kids implant the exclamation point into their long-term memory. While you are out there building marvellous stick and stone exclamation points, you realise that with all these nature inspired exclamation marks lying all over the playground you may as well count them and measure them to satisfy the logical-mathematical learners in the class.

Meanwhile, the musical learners have picked up some sticks from the neatly piled groups of ten and are drumming out a beat. You quickly seize the opportunity and steer them into dropping a stone below each stick as it taps the ground to stimulate that all important visual/oral connection of the image of the exclamation point.

As you head inside dripping sweat and ticking off the multiple intelligences on your fingers you realise that you have missed one. No reason to fret. The social-interpersonal learners, those who are inspired by their relations with other people, can successfully embed the all-important exclamation point into their long term vault by helping out all those unfortunate learners who still think you drew your lower case **i** upside down.

So, about those kids who are convinced they are seeing an upside down *i.* They need a whole other type of differentiation. This is not just about learning styles any more. This differentiation is all about leveling kids according to academic achievement without calling it leveling. We officially stopped doing this back when we dedicated ourselves to inclusive education. We must never-ever let these kids know they are behind. If we tread lightly and are very, very careful, perhaps the 'upside down *i* camp' won't notice that they can't sound out the word *cat* while Rhonda Reader is finishing up the *Tale of Two Cities*.

Back in the 60s when I was learning to read, our elementary school was progressive enough to employ academically leveled reading groups. Despite the teachers' best efforts with fun group names, we still all knew exactly where we stood. The Eagles or Bluebirds read chapter books and clearly outranked the Sparrows or Wrens with the alphabet cards. Kids knew then and they know now.

Advice on differentiation: Just do it!

Field Trips - AKA Excursions

How a teacher views field trips (called an excursion in Australia) has a whole lot to do with her/his tolerance for the unexpected. A quick dipstick to assess your level of tolerance for the unexpected would be to reflect on how you might potentially react to a volcano erupting in your front yard.

If you are the sort of person who would glance out the front door, recognize the growing volcano, grab your fire extinguisher and tackle that pesky lava with confidence and guts, you might just be able to handle a busload of over-excited six-year olds. Now, since this rarely ever happens to most of us (the volcano thing) it is difficult to make a true test using this particular measure. However, you will need to muster up a similar level of coolheaded, can-do attitude to guide your tiny charges safely through an off-site educational experience.

Field trips with kids under the age of about ten are most akin to herding cats. I say herding cats, because herding sheep would be way too easy. People often use the *herding cats* expression without really thinking about what herding cats would actually entail. Anybody who has ever taken even just one cat to the vet in one of those flimsy little cardboard cat carriers has had a little experience, but a herd of cats?

To assist with the cat carrier image if you are not a cat owner, a few years back my husband got a phone call from our son's fiancé. Now mind you this was an international mobile phone call from Australia to the USA. The conversation went something like this. "The cat got out of his box! I can't get him back in! My arms are bleeding!" With an image of the poor girl trapped in a car with a crazed devil cat fighting for his freedom as she (unable to contact anybody else within a nine thousand mile radius) frantically dialled her father-in-law-to-be for advice, my husband was stumped.

Calmly he offered up something lame like, "OK. Not sure what I can do about that from here, but maybe you should just get out of the car." Bailing on a tough situation unfortunately is not an option for a teacher.

I also like to compare the experience of taking primary school kids on an excursion to playing one of those little hand held games we had back in the day before electronics. We used to get these engaging little gems for five cents out of gumball machines or find them in boxes of Crackerjacks or breakfast cereal. They were smaller than the palm of your hand and encased in plastic with a little cardboard insert inside that had tiny holes in it. They usually had a half a dozen metal balls like BBs that rolled around as you tilted it and you had to try to get all of the little balls to each sit in separate holes all at the same time. It was a frustrating game because just when you were about to manoeuvre that last pesky ball into a hole one or more of the others would escape and roll away. That is exactly what it is like to keep kids together on a field trip. Never, ever attempt a school excursion alone.

Collecting the permission slips and money is far and away the most appealing aspect of field trips. It is a well-known fact that all teachers secretly wish they were accountants. However, there would be no challenge in all this high finance if all the parents sent in the signed permission slip and exact amount of money in a sealed envelope labelled with the student's name and event. No, we teachers much prefer being handed sticky fistfuls of random coins while trying to take attendance, do lunch count, answer urgent questions, show appropriate enthusiasm for little Bobby's dangling baby tooth and still get the day off to a calm start. If you are lucky, that fistful of coins turned over to you during this flurry of morning activity might be in a twisted baggie or tattered envelope labelled 'field trip.'

Later in the morning, head in your hands, with all this random coinage on your desk you have to admit defeat and ask, "OK, my little darlings, who gave me some money this morning?"

In perfect synchronisation all twenty-seven kids look at you as if you have dropped the ball and answer, "I did." Of course you did.

Inevitably as you are about to board the bus for the eagerly anticipated field trip, little Bertha will whisper a confession to you. Last time she rode on a bus she threw up all over her shoes. Immediately park this child in the front seat of the bus with the rubbish bin on her lap, but whatever you do don't be a martyr and sit next to her.

As you nervously keep your eye on Barfy Bertha, just a few blocks away from the school somebody will need to pee even though everybody was told to go before you left the school. When you arrive at your destination, Joe will be missing a sock, Sally will have lost her lunch, and you will have already lost your mind.

And, if you think nobody sings, "The Wheels of the Bus Go Round and Round" any more – you are wrong. They can – and do – sing it over, and over, and over. As it turns out there are an unlimited number of verses one can invent for that song. Kids move well beyond the wheels, the wipers, the headlights and the horn as they sing about the different parts of the bus or people and things on the bus and the sounds they make.

Just a couple of my favourites: "The teacher on the bus goes shh, shh, shh – shh, shh, shh – shh, shh, shh." Or "The driver on the bus says, sit, sit, sit…" The little travellers always think they are so clever and original when they come up with those verses. Meanwhile if it is a traditional yellow American school bus with no shocks or seatbelts the kids in the back seats are going bounce, bounce, bounce every time we go over a bump and they are popped up towards the ceiling like human popcorn. Back in my day we incessantly sang, "Ninety-nine Bottles of Beer on the Wall." God forbid a child mention beer or any other evil beverage while getting a public education these days, but I still maintain that at least we were learning how to count backwards with the beer bottle song.

Don't get me wrong, I believe in field trips with all of my heart. Thanks to my own misguided enthusiasm, we had six field trips annually in our first grade classes in Colorado. It had been a long-term goal of mine to have at least a half dozen field trips in one school year. That particular school in Colorado was the only school where I attained that goal. This was due to the fact that I simultaneously had a rookie teacher and another colleague as insane as myself teaching in the same grade level with me. Think about your strongest memories from your school years. Most likely they involve a field trip.

I remember throwing up in one of the tunnels under the Minnesota State Capitol when I was in sixth grade. My oldest daughter remembers being upset on a field trip, because when it came time to eat lunch, her drink had leaked all over her sandwich. Convinced she would surely starve before getting home to a food source, she forced herself to eat the soggy thing at great risk of repeating her mother's vomiting extravaganza. My younger daughter got a tiny shell fragment in her eye as an eleven-year-old on a weeklong school beach excursion and fearing being sent home early, she did not tell the teachers about it and consequently arrived home with an ugly eye infection.

My oldest son got hit by a car in Spain on a high school trip and shrugged it off, so as not to worry anybody. He was already a giant of a person and had probably dented the car when it hit him. He might have got away with concealing the incident except his entire left side was black and blue – a dead give away when we picked him up upon arrival back to Australia. My youngest son returned from a three-day bush camp in third grade with no pillow, socks, hat, or spare underwear. He most definitely had left home with all of those things in his backpack. Mind you, none of these mishaps was specifically mentioned as a risk factor on any of the permission slips.

Despite all the things that can and do go wrong there is nothing like a field trip to stimulate learning. After our trip to the Mining Museum every year in Colorado our first graders found gold, molybdenum, silver and iron ore in abundance on the playground. When we had been to the zoo they saw tigers and gorillas in the forest abutting our school. In the weeks following our trip to a historic ranch they all declared that they were descended from the same Native American woman who talked to them in the tepee. At the Pioneers' Museum they again found numerous folks that were surely their long lost relatives and discovered that the weird contraption seen in Grandpa's garage was in fact a rotary dial telephone. In Australia during an excursion to Parliament House several fourth grade students even learned a totally unrelated lesson about the instability of digestion when they followed up lunch on the lawn with rolling down the grass hill numerous times.

We took our first graders to the zoo every year in Colorado. Despite the cliché this sounds like it truly was a fun excursion. The resident predatory animals looked forward to it too. As we paraded a smorgasbord past their enclosure each year they came over to drool at the fence. The tigers in particular were fascinated by the bite-sized morsels being dangled under their noses just on the other side of some surprisingly thin Plexiglas. The clueless kids in the bunch pressed their little noses up against the glass and said things like, "Oh, he wants to be friends!" However, there were always a couple of kids in the group who were more in touch with their natural primal instincts and stood well back in a defensive fight or flight mode. These kids didn't view the tiger attacking his 'blood popsicle' (blood frozen by zookeepers as a treat) as adorable. They saw it clearly as a cautionary display and hovered close to the teacher.

My favourite part of the zoo trip was watching the collective gait of my tiny charges change after each animal encounter. If we had just observed the wallabies they hopped. If we had seen the elephants they lumbered with hands clasped in front of them swaying like a trunk. If we visited the gorillas their knuckles dragged on the ground. One year the kids were so engrossed in this primate behaviour that half a dozen kids ended up with bloody knuckles. So immersed were they in knuckle dragging that they were oblivious to the skin being ground off their scrawny digits. Woefully short of Band-Aids in my pockets I convinced them all to suck on their fingers. Mmmm, tiny blood popsicles.

Perhaps this altered stride was the cause of a frightening tumble one year. As we were descending an open-grid metal stairway one of my little boys was suddenly tumbling head-over-heals from the landing down to the asphalt about twenty steps below. Luckily for his sake (and my career) Sturdy Stan was a husky boy who will undoubtedly one day be an NFL linebacker. As he splatted at my feet he instantly jumped back up, shook his head and wriggled his arms and shoulders about as he quipped, "I'm OK. I'm OK. Flesh wounds really. Just flesh wounds."

As I staunched his bleeding with the crumpled, but clean tissues I always have at the ready in my pockets Princess Prissy who was now frozen on the landing began to wail and carry on because she was no longer capable of negotiating those terrifying steps after witnessing her classmate's failed attempt. Unfortunately for me a response such as, "Suck it up, Princess," is not appropriate and I had to go make a rescue before all hell broke loose amongst the general populace of the class. Where were my parent volunteer chaperones at this point you ask? How the heck do I know? They were probably imitating turtles with the small group in their charge.

Despite all of the wild and wonderful creatures the students encountered on the trip to the zoo, they were most enamoured by two experiences. First, there were the peacocks that freely roamed the grounds. Undoubtedly, this was because the kids could sense a very real possibility of getting to touch one if only they were wily enough. Despite relentless pursuits, this physical contact never occurred.

The other object of endless intrigue was a fake rock tunnel. This short tunnel was perfectly designed for tiny toddlers to toddle through and teenagers to scrape the skin off their vertebrae. Ducking their heads and donning an expression of anticipated adventure to come, my six-year olds plunged into this two-meter long tunnel and emerged ten steps later giggling with delight. Why this was such a thrill was a mystery to me, but the enthusiasm of the kids was infectious and I just had to crawl through it one year to unravel the mystery. The magic was lost on me along with some vertebrae skin.

As with most field trips the bus ride home from the zoo is always much quieter than the way there. In fact children falling asleep are not at all unusual. What *is* unusual is not waking up upon arrival. One year I had a kiddo who could fall asleep anywhere and anytime. This kid had already fallen asleep several times in class, in the cafeteria, at recess and sitting up during group time on the floor. Medical consultation had found no apparent reason for it and chalked it up as just a remnant of recent infancy. So when he fell asleep on the bus it was no surprise to anybody.

However, this kid was never easy to wake. Seriously, if a kid can sleep outside during recess he is not going to wake to voices calling his name on an emptying bus. I had to practically shake the teeth out of his head to bring him back to us. Picking him up was not an option, because this kid at six years old weighed more than I did when pregnant with my kids. When we finally roused Chubby Chuck he sat up, looked at us with bleary eyes, smiled sweetly and asked if it was lunchtime yet.

Contraband is always a possibility. My all-time favourite field trip incident is a second-hand story. Following a trip to the Australian National Zoo a youngster arrived home with a wriggling lump inside the front of his coat. Intrigued, his mother asked him what was inside his coat. Grinning with delight, the boy flung open his coat to reveal a tiny live penguin! Somehow this intrepid five-year-old had managed to pluck a fairy penguin from the open-air pen, stash it inside his coat, ride the bus back to school, then the family car home - all the while concealing a live penguin! Teacher's due diligence at its finest.

My final field trip story is also a second-hand one. The school where this legendary *fail* originated had made their traditional Aussie excursion to the beach (two hours away) and had by all accounts had a sensational time. They returned home on the bus happily singing camp songs and reminiscing about the good times had by all.

The avid adventurers were greeted in front of the school by an armada of smiling, waving parents. When all children had disembarked, one confused couple remained standing on the footpath enquiring as to the whereabouts of their darling little boy. Yikes! The biggest no-no of teaching – a child left behind. Way behind.

Frantically dialling the Surf Club to see if they still had the little guy, the teachers endured a rightly deserved tirade by the enraged parents. The lifeguards went out to the beach and found the child in question waiting exactly where he had been told. Apparently this obedient child had not heard the follow-up instruction to board the bus.

The continued inaction by this youngster once he discovered he had been abandoned showed amazing patience and lack of curiosity on his part. No biological child of mine would have stayed put that long. Driving back over to the coast with the parents to pick up this wayward student was the last official action of this poor teacher's career.

Despite the considerably increased possibility of the dreaded big three – vomit, injury or missing in action – I believe wholeheartedly in the value of field trips/excursions as an unparalleled learning experience.

Advice on Field Trips:

1. Consider a leash.
2. Suppress panic at all times.
3. Count accurately, recount and then count again.
4. See number 1.

Camps

School camps are the ramped-up version of excursions/field trips. All of the possible scenarios described in the previous chapter can and do happen. The big difference is that they happen for a prolonged period of time and the kids don't go home at the end of the day. At camp kids cry, vomit and giggle incessantly – sometimes simultaneously. If it rains the kids are also wet. Despite depictions of summer camp in movies and popular culture, most American school systems are actually terrified of them. Most Australian public schools on the other hand start taking kids on overnight camps at age eight.

Now let's review the basic characteristics of an eight-year-old. Not only do they cry, vomit and giggle incessantly as stated above. They also have been known to pee the bed, miss their mommy, lose their socks, and wander away. That is the short list.

However, the flip side of the experience is that those same pesky mini people ask fascinating questions, explore with abandon and view the world with awe and wonder. Good for the soul. In fact, overnight camps with primary school aged students could be compared to one of those expensive swanky cleansing retreats that renew your soul. The problem is that the school camp version comes with a teeny bit of sleep deprivation, no silence and an overwhelming feeling that the soul has just been cleansed with steel wool rather than a lavender steam bath.

In my experience the three-day camp seems the traditional norm in Australia and it goes something like this. The children arrive at school the morning of departure with enough luggage to travel across Europe – twice. They can't find the teddy bear they packed and want their frazzled parents to go home and fetch it. They giggle, they cry, and sometimes they vomit. Told you.

Once you count them several times and they board the bus and wave goodbye to their teary parents the real fun begins. I'd like to tell you that the bus ride is the most challenging part of any camp, but it is not. Bats are.

My colleagues and I spent two sleepless nights a couple of years ago trying in vain to convince dozens of squealing nine and ten-year old girls that the micro bats that had just been removed from their cabin were most assuredly the only ones that had made their way inside. Once removed by the camp caretaker these friendly creatures would definitely not return and the caretaker, without a shadow of a doubt, had humanely removed all bats in existence. We even tried to convince them that these tiny bats were adorable little creatures and how lucky they were to have seen such spectacular wildlife up close. Unfortunately, none of this persuasion prevented several tiny stress heads from hovering at our bedroom doorway periodically throughout the night.

Sleep deprivation is by far the toughest part of camp. Humans are not rational in a sleep-deprived state. Children are not rational to begin with. Pair a sleep-deprived teacher with a homesick, exhausted, irrational child and you have the fuel for explosive reactions. Oh, it all starts out lovely enough. We rub a homesick child's back and whisper soothing words. We are patient. We are kind. We are empathetic. Three hours later, after getting out of bed approximately 4,856 times to demand silence of children that we are expressly forbidden to beat, that same darling, sweet, sobbing child arriving in the doorway resembles a red-eyed demon. Lifting our throbbing heads off the pillow and turning our haggard faces towards the distressed child we bellow, "STOP!" with a hand up like a traffic cop. "Go back to bed right now or so help me…"

The sneaky bedside wake up is even worse. Blessed silence has finally descended by about two a.m. No giggles, no crying, no more begging to go home by students or teachers. Aside from the snoring of my colleague in the other bed, peace reigns. Vaguely my sixth sense begins to pick up an unwelcome presence. Cautiously I open one eye. An apparition looms over my bed and tentatively whispers, "Are you awake, Mrs. Davis?"

Bolting upright in bed I nearly knock the scrawny, shivering child off her feet with the flailing of my arm.

"Well, I am now, aren't I?" I grizzle as the frightened child sprints back to bed.

By morning students and teachers alike stumble to breakfast in a judgment clouding fog of exhaustion. Simple requests like, "May I go to the toilet?" or "Are we allowed seconds?" are met with silent dagger-like stares. Plied by the kitchen staff with coffee and extra treats (like actual butter for our toast) the teachers slowly ease towards an acceptable level of polite human interaction. Eventually we conjure up a fabricated version of enthusiasm.

Teachers unaccustomed to exercise limp painfully off on the nature hike or out to manage an outdoor activity that the camp staff has carefully prepared with clear, written 'foolproof' instructions. Desperate to maintain control and offer a sense of fun and adventure the teachers follow orders and trundle off into the trees laden with unwieldy equipment and a group of chattering students in tow. Once well out of contact with the creators of this new and exciting experience and unsure whether they have even found the designated location, the teachers embark on the time-honoured tradition of faking the fun. It is camp after all. If we come back sweating, dirty, smelling like campfire, sticky, muddy, soaking wet, or laughing uncontrollably the activity has been a success.

By the second evening the campers are slowing down somewhat by dinnertime giving the teachers a glimmer of hope. However, with renewed sustenance they rally. They show a level of resilience seldom seen in the classroom. Despite scratches, mosquito bites, missing gear, lack of sleep, some dented egos and sore muscles they vote for an evening dance over a trivia or movie night. They sing (scream), dance (run), and wave (chuck) glow sticks to disco music that has been in the camp activity hall storage cabinet since the early 80s. The teachers smile indulgently while watching the clock diligently and mumbling, "There's no place like home. There's no place like home," quietly under their breath.

Except for the most die-hard of needy students, most of the kids are marginally quiet by midnight on the second night. The teachers sit stoically waiting for peace to reign and vowing once again to not offer any choice on the evening activity next year.

By morning we are on the glory run. A light is twinkling encouragingly at the end of the tunnel. Teachers are cautiously unclenching their core muscles, downing unhealthy quantities of coffee and listening with some grudging sympathy to stories of missing items as students pack their bags before breakfast. A final surge of energy is mustered in preparation for the last activity of this year's camp. With any luck everyone will board the buses home in a couple of hours with limbs intact, minimal sunburn and new stories to tell.

One of my favourite excursions back-in-the-day was the annual fifth grade camp down on the Australian South Coast where the kids learned surf lifesaving, camping skills and participated in team contests. One of the traditional challenges was to build a raft as a team. Each team of six was given six long PVC pipes with the ends stopped up so they would float, several lengths of strong rope and three paddles. The challenge was to build a raft and then paddle it with all six campers on board to the other side of a lagoon and back. The intended outcome was a realisation that teamwork was the ticket to success.

However, the primary goal as far as the kids were concerned was to finish first. It was fascinating to watch each group tackle the task. The winning team one year (all female) had a strong leader who took control, solicited ideas first and then put it to a vote. The team then carefully and painstakingly knotted together a reasonably seaworthy vessel.

Meanwhile, the least successful team tore around like a bunch of chattering monkeys, swinging PVC pipes around, nearly knocking off teammates' heads and snatching bits of rope from each other. This team happened to be predominantly male. They quickly lashed together a jumble of pipes and launched their boat first, paddling frantically as they shouted triumphant taunts back at the shore-bound teams.

Less than twenty-five meters from shore the whole ramshackle construction began to unravel. As each drenched and cussing sailor scrambled to mount a pipe and kick back to shore, the sleek and carefully planned raft of the eventual winners entered the water. Smiling smugly, they saluted their soggy classmates as they glided past. Lesson learned in the 'haste makes waste' category, but maybe not so much gained in humility.

I dare say this marvelous team building activity would look quite different these days. The kids would all be wearing a regulation sun hat, sunglasses, fluorescent safety vests, life preservers and maybe even a tether. When they fell in the water they would have to plough through a slick of sunscreen with little hope of getting a grip on the sunscreen-slathered pipes. Also most likely, the debrief would look less like an analysis of teamwork and construction technique and more like a group counselling session for all the sensitive little losers who couldn't push a restart button when it all went wrong. Hence this activity no longer occurs.

Students are not the only ones having moments of personal growth while on school and sport camps. Teachers grow stronger too. Admittedly some of the teacher growth involves growing less enchanted with their choice of profession. However, there is usually ample opportunity for personal growth involving more concrete experiences. Unfortunately the majority of these experiences seem to involve dangling from ropes high above the ground.

Now I am not afraid of heights particularly, but I don't actively crave these sorts of adrenaline seeking experiences either. I have enough grey hair from watching my own children defy the laws of physics. Technically it is perfectly acceptable for teachers to pass on the physical parts of these adventures, but in the interest of modelling enthusiasm and a can-do attitude, I always have a go.

One year at camp as it was beginning to sprinkle, the nine and ten-year-old kids in the activity group I was charged with supervising convinced me to take a turn on the big swing. However, 'big swing' is not an accurate portrayal of this contraption. It was in fact a rope and pulley setup where the group hauls the swinger skyward and then the swinger chooses when to release and go. The camp guide took great pleasure in egging the kids on.

Theoretically the swinger controls how high she goes by calling out to her crew to stop pulling the rope. Only after convincing my students that it would scar them for life if I peed my pants did they stop my upward ascent. As the sprinkles turned to a full-blown downpour and the first lightning bolts streaked the sky I pulled the release ball to begin my swing. I did this so fast that I hit myself in the face with the back of my own hand. It was definitely worth the bruised cheek. I wished I had let them drag me all the way to the top. FYI – I did not pee my pants.

American teachers are not as big on overnight excursions as Australians. I believe litigation springs to mind. Looks of horror ensue when I speak of the marvellous adventures to be had when you take kids away for overnight or longer. However, despite the hardships encountered by supervising teachers, the possibilities for team bonding and true self-reliance abound in these situations. We get to know our charges on a whole new level. How else would you ever know that Johnny is afraid of ants or tiny Kathy snores louder than a two-ton sea lion? How would you know that Sam has never brushed his own teeth before or Sue walks in her sleep? Staying in a rough-hewn cabin on a mattress made of two inches of compressed and slightly mildewed smelling foam with a dozen or so twelve-year-old girls is not likely to be on anybody's list of preferred scenarios. I was not fond of this idea even when I WAS a twelve-year-old girl. Yet each year I agree to go and each year I am glad I did.

The key factor in your psychological success is to forget sleep. That luxury will not be yours for the duration of the excursion. Even if you are lucky enough to have successfully confiscated all forbidden contraband, squashed all irrational fears, extinguished all flames of passionate hatred towards former best friends, soothed the socially wronged, and convinced them all that there are no bears, dingoes, perverts, or potential boyfriends lurking outside the cabin walls, you are still in for some long nights.

My chaperoning experiences over the years have included high school sports camps as well as coaching or managing travelling athletic teams. Due vigilance is the name of the game with teenagers. Back in the early 80s my husband and I teamed up with a couple of our elite running friends to hold running camps for kids aged twelve to eighteen years old. We held these camps in various bush land retreats outside of Auckland, New Zealand.

The very first night, of the very first day, of our very first two-week-long camp, after conducting a cabin check to make sure all campers were safely tucked away for the night, the four of us were hanging out in our comfy four-bunk adult cabin. Congenially congratulating ourselves on a successful and fun-filled first day, we felt relaxed and content. Suddenly, hearing a muffled noise outside, my husband stood up, slid the curtain aside and glanced out the window. "Well, gosh golly gee!" he exclaimed – or something similar.

"What's up?" the rest of us cautiously queried.

"It seems that we have boys visiting the girls' cabins," was the disheartening reply.

"Well, shucks, that's a bother," we responded in unison – or something similar.

As we hurried to rectify this situation, we realised that the ensuing thirteen days would be a sleep deprived endurance contest with each of us taking a 'soldier at the campfire style' two hour watch detail near the cabin window each night. Bars on the windows and a log nailed to the doors would have been easier, but most certainly against fire regulations.

In Australia during the 90s I had the dubious privilege of going away with teenaged kids as the coach of our state representative athletic teams on several occasions. A particularly memorable trip to Adelaide involved secondary school track and field athletes at the

Australian National Championships. We had finished a particularly successful day at the track and the medal winners wanted to celebrate. However, there were still a couple of days of events to go, so my fellow coach and I made the rounds of all the hotel rooms at about ten p.m. to make sure everybody was settled in for the night.

All was as it should be. So, I hopped into the shower. As I was relaxing under that soothing stream of hot water after a long day at the track a loud and persistent banging on my door suddenly interrupted me. I wrapped a towel around myself and hurried to open the door. My co-coach (I will call him Jeff, since that was his name) nearly fell into the room when I opened the door. Jeff was not much older than most of our athletes and relatively new to the team coaching gig. He had a wild-eyed, yet determined look on his face as frantic words tumbled out of his mouth. They were gone! Most of the older athletes were gone. Gone where?

As it turned out, Jeff had grown up in that town and knew exactly where the young truants might be. I quickly dressed and we headed out to the pub district where the Saturday nightlife was in full swing. Lucky for us we blended right into the scene decked out in our team warm-up suits and driving a fifteen-passenger van. Jeff drove slowly and carefully in a quest not to strike and kill any inebriated underage athletes. As we rounded a corner I spotted our wayward crew strolling along trying to look casual while laden down with several twelve packs of beer and other grog.

In a totally unrehearsed, yet smooth motion I leapt out of the van as Jeff sped around the block in order to pull up beside our young delinquents. As I approached the kids head-on from down the block on foot, they spotted me and froze like deer in the headlights. At that moment I could read their minds as they made the split second decision not to drop the grog and bolt. "Should we run for it? No. Better not. She knows who we are." They remained frozen in place as I closed the gap between us with long, deliberately paced, authoritative strides.

In a perfectly synchronised operation, Jeff pulled up to the curb just as I reached the kids and he flung open the van's side door. I simply commanded, "Get in." They silently filed into the van and sat down with the grog at their feet and their folded hands clenched between their knees. Again, unrehearsed but highly effectively, we rode in absolute silence all the way back to the hotel. When Jeff pulled up in front, I opened the van door and Jeff barked, "Get out."

By the time we had marched them all into one hotel room for their hard earned and fully deserved lecture the work was half done. They were quaking in their boots from the only four words we had uttered, "Get in" and "Get out." By the time we finished our calm and deliberately slow lecture and had assured them that, "Yes – parents would be informed of their transgression," and "No – we did not know the full extent of consequences that would be handed down by the powers that be," the girls all had tears in their eyes and the boys sat with their folded hands firmly clamped between their knees and their heads bowed.

Convinced that we had handled this delinquency in the most professional fashion and everybody was truly sorry they got caught (we weren't silly enough to think they were actually sorry they did it) we asked if there were any questions before we released them to all go back to their rooms. One sincere young man raised his hand and asked, "What are you guys going to do with the grog?" Without missing a beat, Jeff replied that his parents still lived in this town and we would be dropping the offending beverages off at their house the next day on our way out of town and he and his family and friends would be having "one hell-of-a party at Christmas."

Advice on camps:
1. Grow eyes in the back of your head.
2. Bring your own bedding.
3. Caffeine.

Characters

My first graders were happily decorating covers for their work portfolios. Suddenly the serenity was shattered as Aggravating Angie waved her orangutan arm wildly in the air and shrieked, "Teacher! Teacher!" I was a bit annoyed that she was still calling me 'Teacher' after two whole weeks in my classroom, but to be fair I couldn't rapidly recall her name at that exact moment either, so I replied with the same urgent tone, "Student! Student! What is it?" Startled, she dropped her arm, resumed colouring and said with a pout, "Well great! Now you made me forget." Welcome to my world little missy.

Each unique character plays an integral role in your classroom. These endlessly fascinating human beings are the entire reason for your employment and how you respond to their individual needs and dreams determines your level of success.

What follows is just a sampling of a select few of the memorable characters that I have encountered over my decades of teaching. They serve as a small snapshot of the people whose actions or personalities have stuck with me all these years and left a mark on me as a teacher and a person. Since colleagues also influence your ongoing development, I have included some of them as well.

Rolling Boy: RB was a tall, lanky boy who used to roll around on the floor in my sixth grade classroom in a small semi-rural school in Australia. These days he would most likely be diagnosed with ADHD or autism. But back then he was just a kid who rolled around now and again. His classmates didn't seem particularly disturbed by this behaviour, as I am fairly sure they had seen this numerous times over the years having grown up with this kid. He really could have better used his extraordinary height to be the guy who swung from the rafters, or poked holes in the ceiling with a pencil, or put his grimy mitts on all the door jams, but no... he was the guy who rolled on the floor. This was not accompanied by any aggressive, loud, or otherwise disruptive actions. Nor was it alarming after the first time I saw it happen.

Upon enquiry with former teachers and his parents, I was assured he was not having convulsions or any kind of a fit. He also did not have any kind of sensory diagnosis. It seems he just had a personal movement urge. Several times a day he simply stopped sitting, standing or walking and very purposefully and happily laid down and rolled on the floor for a bit – like a euphoric cat twisting around in catnip. It was a relatively harmless little quirk really and his classmates enjoyed all other aspects of his personality so much that they let it slide. The last time I saw this kid, when he was nearly thirty years old and 6'8" tall, he was upright and playing center (quite well) on a recreational league basketball team and he didn't roll on the floor even once.

Ghost Whisperer: GW was a dreamy little girl in my class one year that could talk to ghosts. She had an ethereal look about her and her eyes never seemed to focus completely on you when you spoke to her. Her gaze seemed to be focused through and somewhere behind you. She had some fascinating stories to tell of the various ghosts who had visited her. She was not frightened or at all freaked out by these visits. She simply related her encounters as if she were telling about her cousins coming for a visit. Odd as these stories were, they seemed normal coming from her. It is hard to describe, but if somebody was going to see ghosts it was going to be this particular child. When I mentioned this unusual seven-year-old conversational material to her parents they shrugged it off without concern, saying something profound like, "Yeah, she does that." Who am I to judge what one does or does not see?

Black Hole: Organisational skills are not a hallmark of first graders, but one of my favourite little six-year-olds took this deficit to new and dizzying heights. BH could lose items faster than you could turn around. I could hand him yet another pencil and before I had taken one step he would already be without one. This baffled not only him, but also the students who sat near him. Sometimes classmates became obsessed with finding his math book or journal for him. They just needed to make sense of the vanishing that was happening before their very eyes. Maybe there was some sort of miniature black hole surrounding his seat and school supplies were particularly vulnerable to its pull.

This hypothesis was thrown out the window the day he lost his third pair of glasses when he was nowhere near his desk. We had gone to the library/computer lab and he had forgotten his glasses and his ID/password card. Against all better judgment, I sent him back to the classroom to get them on his own. After all, I had seen them both right there on his desk just before we left the room. It would be an easy find.

Astounding us all, he made it back to the library with both the glasses and the library card in his hand. The black hole had not sucked them into oblivion. High fives for the little guy and celebration time! Too soon. The computer lab opened off the library. By the time BH sat down at his assigned computer in the lab the glasses were gone. It was seriously less than ten feet and the glasses were gone. Where? How? They were never found and we will never know.

I ran into this little guy in the hallway when he was a couple of years older and presumably wiser. His appearance stopped me in my tracks. He had his glasses on his face. He was wearing a button-down collared shirt with all the buttons in the right buttonholes. His hair was neatly combed and there was no food on his face. When I recovered from my shock and was able to form a sentence, I asked him how the year was going so far. "Great!" he beamed. Still impressed by the apparently miraculous transformation, I asked him if his school supplies were now neat and tidy as well. When he assured me they were, I asked him how he was managing such a monumental task. He smiled his coyest smile and announced, "My teacher gave me two desks!" Wow! Why didn't I think of that? Maybe we could rent him a storage locker too.

Lion Lungs: LL came in the form of a very small dark eyed cutie with the lung capacity of a full-grown African lion. She revealed her astounding volume and stamina when we had our first fire drill of the year. I had carefully prepped the kids and told them it was just a drill and nothing to worry about. We had already practiced the routine.

Our school was legendary in the annals of school safety drill compliance. It was the only school I have ever taught at where there was actually total silence as the kids filed out of the school and up the hill behind it. It was a truly surreal experience. Well, this tiny siren child single-handedly threw the whole routine into a tailspin. The wail she unleashed as soon as the fire buzzer went off rivalled the blare of the buzzer itself. The other kids froze in place and stared. She covered her ears, closed her eyes and increased her volume.

This spurred the others kids back into action and as the last of them scurried out via our outside door I scooped up my rigid little human bullhorn and trailed behind them. Whispering calming words in her ear I had her subdued by the time we reached our class gathering spot, but she had successfully seared her voice into our collective memories. I am not sure any of the other classes even knew what had happened, because her pitch so perfectly matched the actual fire siren.

Over the year, with kind and gentle intervention I was able to reduce the volume of her vocal response to events she deemed disturbing. However, she continued to respond with a disproportionate amount of passion to tragedies such as a small rip in her paper or a misplaced water bottle.

Wide Eyed Wonder: Imagination abounds in six-year olds, but some munchkins are on a whole different plane. One such child graced my classroom one year. WEW's mind was alive with characters and scenarios and he could zoom through his own little private portals to and from these worlds at the drop of a hat. Whenever he was telling a story his enormous round eyes were as wide a saucers and his face was animated. One day he came lurching into the room with stiff legs and arms. Fearing some venomous creature had stung him, causing limb paralysis, I cautiously inquired as to what was up. He robotically responded, "I – am – a – zombie." Feigning fear, I told him that I was mildly frightened of zombies. He quickly dropped character, grabbed my arm and began stroking it soothingly as he reassured me with, "Oh no, Mrs. Davis. It's OK. Not a hostile one!" Whew. The hostile ones can really ruin my day.

Junior Biochemist: Keeping with the zombie theme, I thought you might like to know that there will be an effective serum for zombie bites in the very near future. I am privy to this information because I had a very sincere little first grade scientist who accidentally came across this miracle cure while developing a cure for the common cold. His intense bright eyes were nearly bulging out of his head the glorious day when he explained to me that he was "pretty sure" his cold serum was going to work on zombie bites as well. JB cautioned me not to get too excited yet because he wouldn't be certain for a few weeks until it had all been properly tested.

I never got to hear how, or on whom, the serum would be tested, because the principal came over the loudspeaker to lead us in the Pledge of Allegiance and the moment was lost. Knowing it was not appropriate to query further on this top-secret scientific project (seeing that I had been cautioned about said top-secret status) I held my tongue and waited patiently for some definitive results.

Finally a couple of weeks later, not feeling I could wait another day, I discreetly asked JB how the serum was coming along and he said it was just about ready as a cure for the common cold. I expressed my amazement at how he has been able to come up with this elusive vaccine at such a young age. When I asked whether it was going to also work as a serum for zombie bites as he had hoped he said, "Well, I am just not sure yet, Mrs. Davis. You know these things take time."

A few days later, having obviously given my inquiry as to the progress of the zombie serum some thought JB passed on some wisdom and advice that might hold me over until such time as the serum was complete. "Mrs. Davis, since you seemed concerned the other day, I just wanted to let you know that if you hear a hissing that sounds a little like a boiling teakettle that could be a zombie." I asked if he was telling me this to keep me safe until the zombie vaccine was ready. Rolling his eyes slightly at my obvious paranoia, he told me that he was just telling me about it because I 'should be more aware of my surroundings'. I am trying, kiddo – every day.

Pig Pen: PP is actually a composite of several children because every classroom has one (or more) of these exasperating creatures every year. He is the child that can make a mess around the vicinity of his desk within fractions of a second after having sat down. This is a highly refined skill. So fine tuned is the technique that the untrained eye doesn't even realise anything is happening until suddenly there is this debris field extending several feet in all directions from the primary source – Pig Pen's desk.

Remember the character from the Snoopy comic strips? Put the original Pig Pen head to head with one of my homegrown Pig Pens and it would not even be a close contest. When Pig Pen cleans out his desk the sheer volume of paper, pencil stubs, pencil shavings, sandwich wrappings, broken rulers, leaves, twigs, and crumbs that gets pulled out onto the floor defies the laws of physics. I honestly can't conceive of how that could all fit in there.

Every year I decide to watch one of these human natural disasters closely for a day or so. Now either I am not very good at this or there is some sleight of hand happening here, because I still can't tell you exactly what force is in effect. The observation goes a bit like this. I watch this child enter the room via the outside door. His hair is neatly combed, face and hands clean, backpack zipped and strapped on both shoulders.

The first glitch occurs as he walks a slightly irregular path across the room towards the hallway to hang up his coat and backpack. There are a couple of dozen desks and other obstacles – human and inanimate that can distract this child along the way. Yet he progresses seemingly intent on the ultimate destination.

By the time he reaches his desk he has already dropped his coat on the floor and his glasses crookedly dangle from one ear. The disgorged contents of his now unzipped backpack lie like a trail of breadcrumbs between his desk and the hallway coat hooks. He still has his shoes on, but one of his socks is on the heat vent.

His lunch box is dripping some sort of toxic looking liquid on the carpet. His hat is in the sink and his homework is in somebody else's cubby. Did I blink? What happened?

By the time he sits down at his desk he has to shuffle through the folders, scraps of paper, crayons, pencils and markers that have cascaded out of his desk when he hip checked it on his way past. By now one of the little tattle-tales in the class has come to report to me that Pig Pen has stolen her pencil, because he can't find his own. I just give her a new one.

Nobody Home: Again this character could be any number of kids and we are all aware of what the blank stare looks like, but this particular fifth grade child had the capability of tuning out so thoroughly, that I have since been able to tell him this story about himself and he doesn't even remember the months of tutoring we both endured.

For a period of time part of my job was math tutoring for kids who were a little behind. I spent over twenty minutes slowly and painstakingly coaching NH one afternoon. He was a nice kid, but I am pretty sure the expression, 'The lights are on but nobody is home', came into being expressly for him. Although I do have my doubts as to whether the lights were ever actually on in his case, I am quite convinced that this young man was not entirely sure where he was, or even who he was, a great deal of the time. This is not to question his intelligence (which I am convinced actually was quite high), just his grasp on his immediate surroundings.

This particular afternoon, he and I were actually making some progress. The lights were flickering up there in the attic. I guided him slowly and carefully to a successful completion of the problem and then asked him if he understood it better now. He enthusiastically bobbed his head in assent like one of those little bobble head figures in the back window of a car. He had a big grin on his face and a pencil gripped tightly in his grubby little paw. Then in front of my very eyes, the bobbing slowed, the light faded, he looked at me vaguely and responded with, "Wait. What?" I-yi-yi! What did he mean by what? Which part of that whole ordeal had now become a what?

Klepto Kid: Back in my PE teaching days I had a close encounter with the Klepto Kid. His thievery skills were legendary in the hallowed halls of our elementary school. He was also somewhat less than legendary when it came to sporting skills, so my PE equipment had never been in any real peril. Nor was he particularly academic, so my rather meagre stash of office supplies were not a huge temptation either.

However, one day it became evident that KK's reconnaissance skills were on par with his ability to pick a pocket. He managed to clean out my entire stash of snacks from my desk drawer during one PE period without me even knowing he had snuck into my office. The tipoffs were the crumbs on his lips and the empty muffin paper in his hand when I popped into the office to grab a Band-Aid and ran smack into the sticky-handed thief.

Now anybody who knows anything about human nature can tell you that taking a muffin from a PE teacher is a very, very bad strategic move. However, in this case it escalated to the level of a federal crime when I mentioned it casually in the staff room in front of our assistant principal who had given this particular child his ninety-seventh warning about stealing just that very morning.

Now, I happened to have been privy to our experienced and direct assistant principal's lecture techniques when she had once asked a violent child why he had punched another child. When his face turned red and he shouted, "Well, I was just angry!" she calmly looked at him and said, "The jails are full of young men who were *just angry*."

I was expecting a similar straightforward lecture for the Klepto Kid when she brought him back to the scene of the crime for a reflection on his digression. However, the entire intervention was derailed when she couldn't find her glasses, which resided on her head when not being used to read disciplinary referrals. She quickly gave him his ninety-eighth warning and went off in search of her specs. Funnily enough, the spectacles miraculously turned up an hour later in my office rubbish bin. Well played KK, well played.

Leo Learner: Leo was extraordinarily knowledgeable in so many subject areas that it absolutely blew my mind. As with other children 'on the spectrum' he had his particular passions and whenever the subject being discussed hit close to his heart he would spring up and take over the class. It was a small cohort and his classmates were accustomed to these interludes having been in formal schooling with this fascinating fellow for five years. They were not just 'used to' his spontaneous mini seminars, but actually looked forward to them, because he was highly entertaining. He would leap to his feet and gallop to the front of the group. Rocking slightly forward at the hips he would declare, "Well actually..." and be off and running with detailed descriptions, sketching diagrams on the whiteboard and fielding questions from his classmates. His actions were always accompanied by sound effects and his lectures were sprinkled with jokes and imaginative scenarios. He engaged his peers like nobody else ever could or probably ever will. I just sat back and enjoyed the show.

The Phoenix: One of my favourite munchkins of all-time has to be my little Phoenix. This pint-sized, artistic and imaginative six-year-old child had a vibrant, cheery personality. Her glasses were always a bit askew, her socks mismatched, her eccentric clothes were unique and she had the most fantastic ideas constantly pinging around in her tousled little head. She believed in magic, miracles and the very real possibility that she

113

could fly. When she had spare time (or what she assumed was spare time) she would draw. Her subject choices and her view of the world were astounding.

One day she began to draw phoenixes. I immediately recognized the bird she had drawn and asked her why she had drawn a phoenix. She looked up at me in her slightly cross-eyed and unbalanced way and told me she liked to draw them because the phoenix was 'a symbol of hope and renewal' and being in my first grade class made her feel like she could be anything she wanted to be. She was six years old!

I repeat – she believed in magic, miracles, and the very real possibility that she could fly. As a result, the other kids thought she was somewhat weird. Maybe. To me she was pure joy. She appears in a later chapter in this book called *Shining Moments* where you will see how this fabulous child had her moment in the sun and accidentally elevated her status amongst the more conventional munchkins in her class and the entire grade level.

Having been introduced to a small sampling of the characters that have wormed their way into my heart over the years you are now prepped to have a crack at reading the crystal ball. I have moved around too much during my career to be able to tell you whether most of my predictions have been accurate, but I can tell you that for those I do know, I have been surprisingly close to the mark.

So based on the above information here are my best optimistic guesses:

RB has invented and markets a new type of whole body massage chair.

GW runs her own highly successful psychic family reunion service.

BH has developed a prototype for a homing device that can be attached to virtually any object, successfully pitched the plan to a fortune 500 Company, but unfortunately has now misplaced the plans.

LPG sings with a techno band.

WEW and JB are top chemists with a major pharmaceutical company and write Sci-fi books in their spare time.

The PPs of the world feature each week in episodes of hoarders' TV shows.

NH is the CEO of a major corporation.

KK runs the rest.

LL has taken over from David Attenborough and *Planet Earth* tops the charts.

The Phoenix is a songwriter or an artist or maybe… just maybe, a teacher.

One advantage in working at so many different schools over the years is that I have had the pleasure of getting to teach alongside some interesting colleagues. Unusual children often grow up to be unconventional adults.

Hannah Hot Flash: For several years I worked with a principal who was well into menopause and the attending temperature fluctuations that come with this delightful time in a woman's life. Unfortunately for the rest of us, HHF adjusted her internal thermostat by opening and closing outside doors. At staff meetings she would be talking away about some riveting educational issue and suddenly beeline for the door and throw it wide open. Snow would come swirling in and everybody would hunker down at his or her table to wait it out. After about ten minutes of sub-zero indoor breezes she would casually stroll over to the door and close it again. She seemed genuinely oblivious to the thirty or so other people in the room. She was a very put together and considerate person the majority of the time, but when the heat was on, the heat was on.

Witless Wonder: Sometimes we meet people in our lives that defy explanation. I was a grade level teammate with one such woman for a year. I found myself often wondering how she made it to school every day. This woman was in her mid-forties when I knew her and seemingly intelligent. However, her manner of communicating was so bizarre that it was next to impossible to leave a conversation without more questions than answers. It would start out OK, but then go off on a tangent that was just so hard to follow that you left the room not entirely sure she was speaking to you any more.

One day I relieved WW in her classroom while she rushed off for an impromptu meeting with the principal. She had some information up on the board that she had been going over with her fourth grade class. Not sure what I was seeing, I asked the class what they had been talking about. They shrugged and said they didn't have a clue. I laughed and reworded my question as to what subject they were discussing. They replied, "Honestly, Mrs. Davis, we have no idea. We just write stuff down and try to figure it out later when she gives us work time." YIKES!

Pirate Pete: I had the distinct pleasure of knowing Pirate Pete as both a teaching colleague and a teacher for my two youngest children. Now first off, I have to say that anybody who has had *both* of my two youngest offspring as a primary classroom teacher deserves some sort of eternal reward. I assure you that a medal, a plaque or even a bronze statue would not be enough of a prize to properly acknowledge the angst these people endured.

Now, if you happen to be reading this book and you had either of my darlings for a high school class or two, you may be thinking, "Hey what about me?" Well, that stint doesn't really count in my eyes. You may think you had a challenge, but by the time they reached high school our dynamic duo were actually capable of sitting still for more than fifteen seconds, had a tiny bit of a filter and were technically responsible for their own learning.

Pirate Pete on the other hand was the sole reason that these two kiddos learned to love school. He had a whacky sense of humour and knew how to meet kids like my two youngest halfway without them realising he had given them any slack at all.

Pirate Pete had several characters in his repertoire. Of course there was the pirate, but there was also an old granny, a clown, and some sort of dog-like animal to name just a few. The characters all had props and a role to play. He deftly used the characters to suit his purpose at the moment. It was not so much the characters that made him so much fun, but his sense of humour.

I first met him on open-house day when my youngest son was in second grade. I was peeking into desks trying to locate my son's abode by tell-tale signs such as shredded paper or dripping liquids. Pete sidled up beside me and asked if I were looking for my sweet boy's desk. When I nodded wearily, he jerked his head in the direction of a desk sitting by itself next to his teacher desk. Already? It was only the second week of school!

Pirate Pete assured me that it was not one isolated or particularly naughty incident that had landed our son within a handy arm swing of the teacher, but just a genuine desire on his (the teacher's) part to unravel the mystery that was our beloved youngest. What was going on in that seven-year-old's head?

I asked him to please share his findings and he regretfully admitted that he knew of only one activity for sure. Then he smiled one of his infectious grins and declared using a perfect imitation of our son's voice, "Did you know that there are more dots in some of the ceiling tiles than others and in that tile over there, the dots look like a spiky backed dragon?"

Pirate Pete regularly used music to reach kids. He would launch into song to get attention, make a point, and divert inappropriate behaviour. All of this constant vocal activity made their class performances at school concerts an absolute joy. The kids were so comfortable with singing, and it had such meaning to them, that you just wanted to be in his class too. I feel fortunate that my kids benefitted from his tutelage.

CJ (his real name): I was lucky enough to team-teach with another man with a guitar a couple of years ago. CJ even wrote songs to go with our units of study. If I were even a shred musical I would teach with a guitar. Someday when I have learned to clap along with simple rhythms for more than sixteen beats or carry the tune of *Row, Row, Row Your Boat* along with just one other person for all four lines of the song, I will get myself a guitar and teach just like Pirate Pete and CJ.

Another of CJ's many talents was storytelling. He and I were two thirds of a three person Year Four team. We were quite the trio; a thirty-something divorcee (CJ), a twenty-something single mom (Cara) and a sixty-something grandma (me). It worked. We were the dream team. When the three of us were in need of extra admin time, CJ would tell a story to the entire cohort while Cara crunched data and I prepped for the next amazing lesson. CJ once dragged out a suspenseful story about his missing cat for approximately three weeks. Told in ten minute instalments, the magic of his storytelling so enthralled the kids that they had no idea that there was virtually no plot. This talented man writes songs and sings in local pubs on evenings and weekends and the crowd often includes students who have dragged their parents along for the fun.

I have taught well over a thousand students in my career and worked with hundreds of colleagues. We have shaped each other in countless ways.

My husband, Peter works in the sporting world and for several years he worked for a national institute of sport. In addition to the coaching and sport science provided at this institution at that time, there was also a live-in athlete component and as a result there were many athletes on campus every day. Peter worked with one scientist who often griped, "This would be a better place to work without the bloody athletes around here all the time." How wrong that cranky fellow was. It is the people that make a place worthwhile.

So, my advice on coping with all the characters (big and small) whom you will encounter:

1. Don't over-analyse anybody. They are who they are. Accept and cherish.
2. Look around at the adults in your life. They all started out as kids.
3. Look around at the kids in your classroom. They will be the adults who run this world one day. Embrace their uniqueness and imagine the future!

Annoying Habits

Children can have incredibly annoying habits that have the potential to drive you round the twist if you let them. Sometimes the aggravation is so constant you have to do everything in your power not to have an overreaction. These habits can include but are not limited to pencil tapping, humming, paper scrunching, touching everybody, sleeve sucking, flipping, flapping, fidgeting and so much more.

I am fully aware of the need for stimulation, self-soothing, more sensory input, less sensory input, movement urges, oral fixations, etc. I have attended conferences and workshops, taken online professional development classes and participated in numerous collegial discussions and online forums. This ongoing professional development and my own teaching experiences have increased my understanding and empathy for these kids. I am not immune to having a few issues of my own. However, all of this empathy does not change the fact that these actions are disruptive to learning and downright annoying.

Not only are young children unconcerned with causing disruption to the learning environment, but the younger the child is, the less aware they are of how their actions are perceived by others. In most cases, even if they have some concept of which behaviours are within social norms and which are not, they really don't care. Some kids have honed the more indirect irritating habits to an exact science and are capable of executing them with such stealth that the teacher's quest to find the perpetrator can become all-consuming.

Take beavers for instance. Every year I have a beaver. The tell-tale signs usually appear after just a few days of school. A truly industrious beaver can fully tenderize that smooth glossy paint on half a dozen yellow number two pencils in a school day. With a bit of dedication to his craft your beaver can actually chew the metal eraser band into tiny bits of unrecognizable scrap metal and spit those miniscule mineral remnants into sinks, pencil receptacles, desktops, floors and any other handy surface. Like an actual beaver you never ever see this happening. You only see the aftermath.

If kids are young enough their residual oral fixation can interfere with full engagement in learning. The temptation to put things into their mouth is just too irresistible. Sometimes it is a strong chewing urge, but often it is just an absent-minded reflex to taste or actually consume an item.

Sleeves are a favourite chewing and sucking target, because they are just so handy. Most of the time this seems to be a male habit, but girls are increasingly drawn to this convenient chew toy. These kids hand you papers dampened by contact with their soggy sleeves.

For some reason the sleeve suckers seem to have a more than average desire to throw their drenched arms around your neck. If the child has resisted sucking for a little while the sleeves will dry and then you just have crusty edges to deal with. If you live in colder climates the wet sleeves freeze at recess. The sleeve suckers come back inside, sit down at their desk and their wrists clunk against the desk top.

Eating glue is an all-time classic. Teachers have abhorred this disgusting habit since the dawn of institutionalized education. This food source has most definitely declined in popularity, so teachers today don't see as much of this as in the past. Mostly this has to do with the glue itself. When I was a kid we used paste, which was actually quite appealing as a foodstuff. It came in a bottle about the size of a baby food jar and had a screw top. When you unscrewed the lid there was a paddle attached to it with which you scooped out globs of paste. The action here was so similar to scooping out peanut butter or vegemite from a jar that the natural next step was to stick that little paddle straight in your mouth. Now once this substance reached the mouth it was usually deemed 'not bad' by the tongue, because it had a slight salty taste and smooth creamy texture (so I have been told). These days, kids have glue sticks or liquid glue that is much less appealing, but not entirely undoable.

At the top of the heap in the readily available snack category for many generations now are the ever-popular boogers. Some children consume this delectable treat surreptitiously, but most kids extract the greenish-yellow delicacy on the tip of their finger and then examine it for at least a few seconds before popping it into their mouth. In the primary grade levels this is so common that it goes virtually unnoticed by classmates. Thank God, in my experience so far, none of my sharing and caring little darlings has ever offered to share with a friend.

If left unchecked these habits can evolve over time into slightly more socially acceptable versions of the original habit by the time the kids are adults. A baby beaver can graduate to chewing tobacco, fingernails, or massive wads of gum. Unfortunately the orally fixated may also move on to a pipe, cigars or cigarettes. The eaters of glue, boogers, or anything stray they found on the floor will spend their adult years seeking the best weight loss programs. So, in addition to curriculums that are longer and more involved than the Magna Carta, we are obliged to also civilize the feral ones in hopes of curbing these habits.

The mouth is not the only instrument of torture employed by these innocent looking cherubs. ADD, ADHD, OCD, ODD; whatever the designation, distractors abound in classrooms. These days we give kids wiggle seats, balance balls, squishy balls or fiddle toys to manipulate in hopes that these devices will keep them from manipulating their classmates. The trouble is that the anti-irritating device can become as irritating as the original distraction. Wiggle seats rarely stay under bottoms and balance balls have so much more potential than merely pretending to be furniture. Therapy putties work their way into carpets. Squishy balls and fiddle toys are, after all, toys.

Destruction and hoarding are habits that can begin early in life. When combined, these habits can create havoc in a classroom. One day in a moment of complete frustration I removed everything from Destructor Hoarder's desk. At this particular school, students had the sort of desks that have an opening like a little shelf just under the writing surface where students can store all their school supplies. This human shredding machine had mangled or destroyed everything in his desk and then added half eaten foodstuff. Daily mixing of this concoction had created a substance with a toxicity level which would most likely be unacceptable according to World Health Organisation standards.

So, at risk of contamination and without a facemask or proper vaccinations, I delved into this miniature hell hole and pulled everything out. After bleaching DH's desk inside and out I left him with just one pencil and a sheet of paper to write on and calmly redirected him to the assignment at hand. By the time I had deposited the bag containing the contents of his desk behind my desk for later sorting and decontamination he had managed to jam the upper part of his body as far as he could into his desk and all we could see were his twitching legs pushing off the floor trying to get further inside.

"Whatcha lookin' for little man?" I queried.

"My banana," he whined.

Seriously? You just watched me scoop everything out and spray the area down with forbidden toxic bleach. Do you really think I left the banana?

One of my major pet peeves is when students wander about while eating. In most American schools kids eat lunch in a cafeteria, which comes with its own set of issues, but in most of the Australian schools I have taught in kids eat on benches outside. Getting them to sit politely and eat with quiet conversation is a mammoth struggle. Apparently this is not the norm in most households any more. Each year I begin again, teaching this most basic of life skills to children who have been feeding themselves for a decade already.

These days we don't make kids sit in their seats working silently, but that doesn't mean that humming, wandering, and random mouth noises aren't still just as irritating to the other kids and the teacher. These actions are difficult to change by the time a kid is around ten years old, because they have become habit.

Advice on habit mitigation:

1. Pick your battles.

It All Begins With Kindergarten

After thirty-three years of teaching, kindergarten was the one grade at the primary level that I had not yet taught as a classroom teacher. I had substitute taught these little mini humans and I had taught them in specialist roles for PE and for science and technology, but I had not been their primary source of enlightenment. My gratitude to this special breed of teacher was without measure. So naturally, I asked to be transferred to kindergarten.

Kindergarten teachers are the first contact with civilization for some of the feral creatures that land on a school's doorstep. Teaching kindergarten was my personal Mt. Everest. I felt that by teaching first grade for four years I might have reached base camp, but the ultimate challenge for me was to summit my mountain. To do this I would have to strap on my crampons and become a kindergarten teacher.

Kindergarten teachers are the ultimate multi-taskers. They were charged with taming these tiny beasts and bringing some order and structure to their lives. Parents may take offense at this view because they feel their tots are perfectly well behaved. Well, yes perhaps they are – within their home with only a couple of siblings. My sister aside (she has thirteen kids) most children are not entering these hallowed halls with a whole lot of group experience. Even if they have attended a preschool, the groups are not large there and they are not expected to line up, sit down, listen and take turns continuously.

Aside from Arnie S, most kindergarten teachers are female. These women were my heroes. In my four-year stint as a first grade teacher I was the direct recipient of their handiwork and my gratitude was immeasurable. There is a popular saying that, 'Everything you really need to know in life, you learn in kindergarten'. As far as personal relations go, this is mostly true. This is when children learn patience, negotiation skills, sharing and taking turns. Teachers diligently teach these skills and then parents (and I include myself in this category) unwittingly try our best to undo their handiwork.

Just when little Johnny has the whole sharing thing down pat we go and enrol him in peewee soccer. We aggressively dash up and down the sidelines every Saturday as the kiddies play clump-ball bellowing, "Take the ball away from him! Don't let him have the ball! Take it away!" When little Johnny stops in his tracks to try and process this instruction, which is in direct violation of the rules so firmly established over the past several weeks by the new love of his life (his kindergarten teacher) we panic. He appears to have lost focus, so we gesture violently with our foot, acting out just how the little tyrant should take the ball. Surely we, his loving and kind parents, can't actually be expecting him to just take the ball away from this perfectly nice kid who seems to be enjoying it right now? What would his kindergarten teacher think?

Despite parents' best efforts to undermine the system, the kids do learn the established norms within the confines of their new daytime abode fairly quickly. They walk down the hall with one hand on their hip and one on their lips, studiously chanting in their heads, "Hips and lips. Hips and lips." They tattle relentlessly on the playground when a classmate steps even a centimetre out of bounds or drops an oat from their granola bar onto the pavement and doesn't pick it up.

They flamboyantly hand each other toys and use a stage voice as they say, "Here. You have it. I will play with something else."

Masking her confusion at being handed a toy she wasn't even mildly interested in, the recipient of such caring and sharing plays the game and with a glance over her shoulder to make sure the teacher is watching she replies, "Thank you. Would you like to be included in our game?"

As the school year wears on some kids may grow weary of the charade and slip back into more comfortable behaviours, but the groundwork has been laid and the foundation of the lingo is there to stay. My personal favourite and one that carried strongly on to first grade and beyond at my Colorado school was, 'You get what you get and you don't throw a fit'. The first time I heard this mantra was when I realised (as I was about to pass them out) that I had received the wrong fourth grade math test papers back from the printer. I muttered out loud, "Sh…oot. This is not what I wanted."

One of my fourth graders quickly admonished me with, "Mrs. Davis! You get what you get and you don't throw a fit." In response to my glare, the cheeky kid added, "Mrs. B said so."

Despite our best efforts, it is easy to misinterpret the intentions of our more unruly munchkins. The vast majority of the time they are not trying to be naughty, rude, or disrespectful. They simply do not have a firm grasp of the expectations yet. Learning school specific vocabulary and traditions can be a bit like learning sport jargon. Case in point; a kindergartener in my PE class took off from second base during a kickball game and sprinted off the school grounds headed towards the nearby houses. Returning to my frantic whistle, he explained himself. He had run because his classmates had yelled at him to, "Run home!"

Sometimes for kindergarteners it isn't just the jargon or expressions that they struggle with. They often have a very literal interpretation. Struggling to explain a new concept to my fledgling group of kindergarteners in my first term on the grade level, I decided to go back to the beginning. I took a breath, smiled indulgently and sighed, "OK, let's just back up." Obediently, the entire group shuffled back on the floor.

Years before I was a kindergarten teacher I was on playground duty one day and had to wait for a dawdling kindergarten boy to stand up from his sand play and walk up the hill back to class after the bell had rung. I have to admit I was less than patient. I had already called out to this kid twice and then I had to trudge all the way down the hill to retrieve him. When I reached the stubborn little guy I asked him his name and why he wasn't coming when he was called. He looked at me, but continued to ignore my request. I told him he was being rude. I then took his hand and led him up the hill to his class. He seemed unperturbed by this and happily accompanied me.

I handed him off to his teacher and told her what had happened. She lifted his chin, looked him in the eyes and asked, "What have you done with your hearing aid?" With a cheeky grin he reached in his pocket and produced it. Now I felt rude. The teacher assured me that it didn't matter what I had said, because she was quite sure he hadn't heard me anyhow.

So it turned out this kid happened to be deaf. This ability to be in one's own little world is not the exclusive realm of the deaf. Almost every kindergartener is capable of entering fantasyland at any time. At times this can be irritating, but it can also work in your favour. If reality is a shaky concept you have so much more to work with when creating fun 'learning engagements'. Imagine if you could ask your colleagues to just pretend to be a frog when you wanted them to jump into a new challenge with enthusiasm. Works like a charm when learning to skip count.

Crying is the biggest stumbling block in the first few weeks of kindergarten. A crying child doesn't learn well and a crying teacher doesn't teach well. Crying is to be avoided. I am happy to report that my first week as a kindergarten teacher involved no crying in my classroom. The only crying occurred outside – from parents. Therefore the trick appears to be to keep the parents outside.

So, with no crying, a limited use of jargon, and a gentle introduction of expectations the kids are ready to begin the business of learning to read and count. Honestly, this is the easy part! People love to compare kids to sponges, lumps of clay, empty vessels and other equally condescending descriptions. They are so much more.

The growth that occurs during the kindergarten year is nothing short of magic. Kids who may not even be able to identify the letters in their own name coming into kindergarten most often leave reading and writing simple sentences. As a teacher, I am not filling a vessel or shaping clay. I am simply watering a seed, which then blooms into a beautiful flower! The seed already held all the potential it needed. All I did was nurture it. The key to all this growth is to pay attention. Watch, listen, learn, and react to student needs. Take delight in who they already are!

Whoa! I got a bit gushy there. Remember that whether or not these little kids learn to read during their kindergarten year, they have taken their first steps. Our challenge is to give them a good beginning. School is not a natural state of being. This first year they are really learning how to DO school.

In my opinion, *time* is the biggest issue in kindergarten. Teachers who move to a role as a kindergarten teacher after spending the bulk of their career in the upper grades go through a painful process of scaling back their expectations of what can be accomplished in a half an hour. A short list of things that can potentially take a half an hour or more for a five-year-old to accomplish includes: tying their shoes, writing their names, getting a drink, going to the toilet, washing hands, eating a strawberry. To be a kindergarten teacher is to wait, and wait, and wait.

Armed with my personal perspectives on the glory and honour of teaching kindergarten, I am happily negotiating my third year as a kindergarten teacher at the tender age of sixty-four years old. May the force be with me…

Thoughts on kindergarten:

1. Take this job only if you have had a full physical and psychological check-up.

2. Bow deeply in appreciation each and every time you encounter a kindergarten teacher. We think we deserve it.

3. Marvel at the little miracles that happen every day in kindergarten.

Kiss and Go

At most schools teachers take turns with the dubious privilege of greeting kids in the morning and seeing them off in the afternoon. This is called car duty. The optimist's view is that before and after school drop-off and pick-up duty can be a great opportunity to become further acquainted with the school community. A lot can be learned about family priorities, time management and the level of comfort a family has with other humans viewing (and possibly handling) their property.

Potential hazards await you when you open a car door to let a child in or out. Here is a partial list of items that have actually spilled on my feet when I have opened a car door during before or after school car duty: empty soda cans, open soda cans and their sticky contents, beer bottles, dirty socks, rocks, sticks, wadded up paper, dried up donuts, styrofoam coffee cups, coffee, juice, other unidentified liquids, marbles, soccer balls, dogs, newspapers and stuffed toys. Cigarette or marijuana smoke haze is the worst. Unlike the projectile vomit of a baby or a slobbery dog's lick, which can be dodged if you are quick enough, smoke haze just rushes right out, surrounds you and then lingers in your hair and clothes.

The drop-off/pick-up area out the front of my school in Colorado was fondly dubbed the Kiss and Go. The school was set at the end of a dead end road with only one way in or out. The line began to form at least a half hour before the end of the school day. These folks were the people who clearly had the most important lives and waiting a half hour upfront was infinitely better than ten to fifteen minutes waiting behind the plebs.

The designated car lane alongside the school sidewalk was clearly marked with bright orange cones. The routine was highly structured and expectations were set high. However like any well-intentioned safety measures, there were gaps – chiefly the gaps between the ears of the intended protected ones and their frazzled parents.

Mild-mannered-me became a dictator with an overused whistle whenever I pulled after school car duty. As soon as the children left the building, no matter how well-mannered they may have been during the day, something tripped in their brains and they scuttled about in the trees and bushes that separated our building from the street, climbing low walls, leaping benches and swinging backpacks over their heads like lariats. Since 99.9% of the parents were in a hurry to drive the fifty meters back home and had been waiting in a line that stretched past their own driveway for half an hour already, they were not in a great mood when they spotted little Suzie playing chimpanzee off the pine boughs.

The procedural vision goes like this. Three cars at a time pull up between the row of cones and sidewalk. Little Suzie, who has been watching intently for Mommy, walks quickly (with her backpack securely positioned on both shoulders and her hands and feet to herself) to the curbside and waits patiently behind the yellow line. The footman (teacher) opens the car door valet style. Little Suzie enters the car, turning her head slightly to thank the footman before politely greeting her mother. The footman closes the door as the mother also expresses her thanks. Then Suzie buckles her seatbelt and they roll smoothly out of the parking lot.

In reality, Mama lurches bumper car style into the parking lot like she is driving a manual shift car for the first time. Her mission is to nab little Suzie as fast as possible and get to yoga before all the borrowed mats are gone. She is scanning the writhing mass of miniature humanity for her little miscreant as she nearly runs over the only family game enough to use the actual crosswalk to get to their parked car. Gesturing frantically at the footman to summon her offspring from the trees, she finally rolls down the window and bellows the crazy monkey's name. Little Suzie, startled from her branch by the totally unexpected arrival of her mother in this place and time, drops to the ground and begins searching for her belongings.

By now all the cars lined up behind Mama Chimp have begun to overheat and Mama is becoming aware for the very first time that she is not, in fact, the only one waiting to pick up a child. Suzie finally arrives at the car, dragging her brand new faux fur coat through the dirt, with papers spilling out in a trail behind her. Mama Chimp's tirade begins as the footman gingerly closes the door and sarcastically murmurs, "You're welcome," through a teeth-clenching smile.

Mama Chimp checks her phone (again), and then peels out of the parking lot while screeching, "Suzie, sit down! Seatbelt!" The footman takes a deep breath and starts over with a fresh smile for the next bumper car.

I have a very solid idea on how to fix this situation. I truly feel that far too much time and effort is being focused on perfection here. Please reference the previous chapter where the children were taught in kindergarten that, "You get what you get and you don't throw a fit." Surely this is a life lesson that would serve everyone well at the Kiss and Go. If parent and child have not worked out some way to recognize each other and the vehicle they commute in *every single day*, then perhaps they should just get what they get and don't throw a fit. Open the door, put the requisite number of kids in each car, close the door and wave them off. We could be done with the whole sordid affair in less than ten minutes! Nobody in all my years of teaching has ever given my plan a chance.

My advice:

1. Wear rubber boots on car duty.
2. Take deep calming breaths.
3. DO NOT punch anybody in the face.

Testing

Standardized testing is widespread and becoming more pervasive every day. To me it seems to be at loggerheads with differentiation. There is nothing standard about kids. Yet, while we are all busy differentiating our instruction we still continue to test kids as if they think and act the same. At the kindergarten level these assessments are all one-on-one with the teacher requiring a couple of weeks of every term to complete. Meanwhile the rest of the class is involved in 'self directed' learning activities. Of course none of these kids would dream of interrupting during a classmate's golden twenty minutes. So, let's delve into the wonderful world of assessment.

In American schools in the primary grades we relied heavily on some very research based and revered assessments. Most of these activities are great learning tools, but as timed assessments they don't tell us anything we don't already know. Some veteran teachers I know fondly refer to one such test as the 'stutter' test. It goes like this: "I am going to say a word and you tell me the sounds you hear in the word." So, the teacher says *Sam* and the kid stutters back S-A-M. We do this as fast as we can for one full minute. If the kid can't stutter fast enough he/she gets some remedial help to get better at this vital life skill.

Another winner is the Letter Naming Fluency test. This also is a timed test in America. My first experience with this test was when my second child (the one her siblings all refer to as the smart one) could not name even half of the letters on this test in kindergarten, yet she was reading above the fifth grade level. Luckily her teacher was about one hundred and seven years old and had been teaching for at least eighty of those, so she was not concerned. She just pointed out to us that this letter deficit qualified her for some remedial help, which (with our permission) she would be inclined to politely decline. We concurred.

Recently a child in a colleague's class was taking this letter naming test and as she pointed to each new letter the darling little guy read, "m, m, m, m, m . . ." When the minute was up he looked up and said, "Boy that sure was a lot of m's and they all look different." Now maybe this kid could do with some of that intervention.

My personal favourite is the Nonsense Word Fluency test. This test is also timed for one minute and kids read the fake words as fast as they can. The idea here is that, because they are nonsense words, you can ascertain whether the kids are sounding out words well or simply recognizing them. This is also a great teaching tool. It is also a decent assessment, but asking kids to do this as fast as they can is just unnecessary pressure.

In my opinion the only redeeming factor of this test was that we used to practice this skill using letter cubes. The students would roll two consonant cubes and a vowel cube. They then arranged the letters into a nonsense word and read it aloud. Sometimes they rolled combinations like F-U-K. It was quite entertaining. Especially if you didn't see the letter combo before the kid did and they went ahead and read it and shouted it out loud. This happened one day just as the principal popped into my room while giving a building tour to the board of education. They were impressed.

Preschool screenings are the best. I remember a preschool-aged neighbour girl who used to sit under a tree and read chapter books to herself and then discuss them in detail with anyone who would care to listen. After her seemingly successful preschool screening she was declared too immature to start school. The reason given was that during the testing she sucked her thumb between tests. Horror of horrors – a four-year-old child sucking her thumb.

Back in the early 90s my four-year-old nephew was sitting for one of these preschool screenings and the tester had given him a pile of blocks. She proceeded to ask him to do various different tasks with the blocks. Dutifully he built each new configuration. Finally he sighed in exasperation, pushed the whole pile back at her and bargained, "Tell ya what. You decide what you really want me to do and *then* I'll do it." Smart kid.

My own wiggly youngest took a similar exam and I am fairly certain that at no point did he sit still for even a millisecond. He squirmed under the table, onto the table, under his chair, in and out of his sweatshirt, never once making eye contact with the tester, but he nailed the block formation every time. To my astonishment they deemed him eligible for early start, much to the dismay of his weary kindergarten teacher who was not at all impressed by his perpetual motion, climbing and jumping abilities, and lack of apparent interest in the alphabet or numbers.

All this testing usually doesn't tell us anything we couldn't figure out after ten minutes of talking and reading with the child. Give me a kid and a simple book and I can tell you exactly what I will need to do with that child.

Testing advice:

1. Jump through the hoops, but don't take it all too seriously.
2. Trust your gut.
3. Don't label a kid just because he doesn't see the point in the test.

Comments on Student Reports

Quite possibly nothing takes more time and thought than teacher comments on student reports. There is a delicate balance that needs to be reached between keeping parents happy and telling the truth. These days most school principals tend to strongly encourage 'positive language' and frown on accurate blunt language. As a parent you generally can read between the lines, but it still feels better to have a teacher write that *Johnny is encouraged to keep his voice at an acceptable level* rather than having the teacher actually record in print for posterity that *Johnny is loud and obnoxious*. Back in the 60s when I was in school the teachers generally told it like it was. If Joe was a bully, they said so. If Sally never contributed, she wasn't deemed insecure or shy, she was told to speak up. These days comments need to be handled more discreetly.

When our younger daughter (the feisty one) was in year two in Australia her teacher was tripping all over his tongue trying to tell us about our beloved little darling at a parent/teacher interview. He explained that, "She is sometimes forceful in her opinions… tends to steer others into doing things her way… someday these qualities will help her to be successful… she is showing promising leadership qualities."

After watching him squirm and struggle to come up with other suitable euphemisms for what he really wanted to say we looked him in the eye and said, "You are trying to tell us she is bossy, aren't you." In response to his rather tentative nod, we assured him that we were painfully aware of that little trait and told him to please feel free to pass on any successful strategies he may come upon for toning her down a notch.

I actually first saw the 'leadership skills' of the Feisty One in action in a public school setting when she was only in preschool. I had gone to help out one morning at the public preschool and the teacher came over to speak to me. She asked me to come have a look as she let the kids out the door to play. I told her I would be there in a few minutes when I had finished cutting up the fruit for morning snack. The teacher insisted I come watch immediately as she let the kids out.

Right there at the doorway stood my little sweetheart looking like an angel and barking like an army sergeant. "You! You're on swings today. You! You're on monkey bars. You two can be on the slide." Whoa!

Slightly embarrassed, mostly impressed and not at all surprised, I turned to the teacher and asked, "Every day?"

To which she replied, "Yup. Easiest year I have ever had."

Comments delivered in person can be handled slightly differently than those written on a student report card. In person comments can be delivered with a kind and loving expression and prefaced with any good qualities you can manage to dredge up to soften the blow. Written comments are just out there hanging like text messages with no visual clues, facial expression or lead-in niceties to slide them by.

When it comes right down to it, most parents know their child and will catch any little nuances you might send their way, so you can avoid spelling out every little fault right there in black and white. Just as we always knew 'leadership' for our youngest daughter meant 'bossy' we also knew 'eager and active' for our youngest son meant, "He can't sit still to save his life." One year our youngest son's teacher wrote, 'improving organisational skills'. We immediately knew that meant he had found his pencil two days in a row.

I'm sorry to report that those organisational skills did not move much beyond the pencil finding competency despite family and future teachers' best efforts. However, this wild daredevil has grown up to be a successful, qualified stunt man. We need to encourage and celebrate each child's unique talents!

Our two youngest kids constantly tested the creativity of the saints that taught them. 'Enthusiastic and energetic child', meant, 'Your child is going to be the death of me... or himself". The proverbial 'contributes enthusiastically to class discussions' meant, 'can't, or won't, shut up'. Parents can take heart in the fact that some of the attributes that are deemed most negative in an educational setting can actually serve a person well in the real world.

Our two older children did not properly prepare us for the face-to-face conferences requiring humility that we experienced with the younger two. The first two were the sort of kids that we all wish we had a classroom full of. Good readers, polite, kind, organised, friendly, respectful, etc. My husband and I strutted around with our chests puffed out waiting for the *Parent of the Century* medals to be pinned to our lapel.

Then along came the younger two, serving up humble pie. Suddenly the teacher's warm handshake, wide smile, and inviting attitude were replaced with a nervous twitch, guarded expression and gun-shy demeanour. We found it easiest to front load the session with assurances that we were fully prepared to hear the truth.

The truth can be as difficult to deliver as it is to hear. Thank God for our boundary pushing youngest pair for giving me a parent's perspective when I deliver the news that little Johnny really is having some challenges with following the rules. I find it especially difficult because some of the little rascals that give me the most trouble are dear to my heart, because of their vibrant personalities. Vibrant personalities or not, parents need to be brought on board to help curb the annoying behaviours and bring out the best in the little darlings. Much as we want kids to have confidence, good self-esteem and a burning desire to learn, we also need to let parents know what is truly happening within their child's academic and social world.

The difficulty for teachers is that the current practice in most schools is to mandate that teachers make content specific comments and that negative comments must be sandwiched with a positive at the beginning and the end. On top of that, the expectation is that we write personalized comments that also fit a standard formula. Confused? Me too.

Report card comments have gone full circle during my career. Gone are the days of "Good work Johnny!" For a while we had free rein to say whatever we wanted to say. Then came computers and in the interest of taking full advantage of this new technology they provided us with a drop down comment menu. A teacher could choose from five standard comments ranging from Susie excels in this subject to Susie is working below grade level. The impersonal approach didn't last long and now we're back to writing our own.

So, assuming the pendulum will swing back soon and we can write just words or phrases again, here are some standard report card comments to help get you started. The beauty of this short method is the vast scope for interpretation. I have provided the true meaning to help you out with those tricky kids:

Acceptable Comment	True Meaning
Friendly and social	Never shuts up
Affectionate	No sense of personal space
Energetic and enthusiastic	Drives everybody crazy
Improved organisational skills	Found his pencil two days in a row
Nice girl	I don't know her
Helpful	Suck up
Needs work on persistence	Quitter
Continues to improve	Not even close yet
Concepts are difficult to grasp	Clueless
Creative ideas	Weird kid
Thinks outside the box	Totally off the wall
Makes interesting connections	Gets way off subject
Readily shares experiences	I know stuff about you

Parent/Teacher Conferences, Interviews and Learning Journeys

Parents think that conferences (called parent-teacher interviews in Australia) are all about teachers sharing how the students are doing, but in actual fact we teachers gain some immensely useful information from these relatively brief encounters. Mind you, both parties come into these meetings with a fair store of prior knowledge about each other, albeit somewhat questionable in its reliability due to the age of the informants.

At conference time we teachers get to meet parents that we have a fairly high curiosity about. We may have met them at back-to-school night, but we don't really know them. I fully realise that what I say in the classroom often goes home and is re-told at the dinner table. Like a good game of telephone the original intent of my words may not be intact by the time this sharing occurs. The same is true with the flow of information from the home front.

Many elementary schools in America have the mind numbing practice of having conferences starting immediately after the kids leave for the day on a school day and continuing until eight p.m. This is followed by conferences from eight a.m. to eight p.m. the following day. The teacher is left at a disadvantage when it comes to quick thinking – as in *who* somebody is when he or she walks into the room. This leads to an impromptu game of recall in which every story, visual clue, gesture, voice inflection and pattern of movement plays a role. A certain percentage of kids are carbon copies of their parents. Some have such perfectly synchronised mannerisms that you are pretty sure you just slipped into a time machine and you are seeing the little kiddo all grown up.

Clothing may provide clues as to a genetic match. If tiny Tina bops into the classroom every morning in a miniature hooker outfit, chances are the woman in the skin tight miniskirt, blouse she outgrew in the sixth grade and the smoky eyes look, is tiny Tina's mom. Likewise when Bubba's dad walks in with his baseball cap on backwards, a wad of chew in his cheek and his pants sagging nearly completely off his backside, you are not even mildly surprised.

Often when a parent saunters, slumps, bounces, stomps, skips, or strides into the room you have your first clue. A spring in the step reveals a confidence that they are about to hear good news. Either that or they are oblivious to just how things really are going. The ones who slink in, edging along the wall in hopes they won't be detected are definitely expecting bad news. These elusive creatures also may have a bit of a defensive posture going on with arms crossed or one forearm up in front of their body as if to fend off blows.

After introductions, the banter begins. The more uncomfortable the conversation is likely to get, the longer the banter. "Say, that thunder shower this afternoon was quite something wasn't it? We sure do need rain round these parts don't we? How about those Yankees? Now, about little Susie."

As the conference continues, some revelations may come to light that help explain some of the unacceptable behaviours on display in the classroom. These little titbits often are revealed in a casual, "Oh, by the way..." fashion. Here is a sampling of the burdens that some of my young students have had to deal with over the years: Sally met her daddy for the first time this summer when he got out of the state penitentiary. Johnny's mom (who moved out three years ago) changed her phone number, because she doesn't want the boys bugging her by calling her all the time. Kelly's big sister ran away last year and hasn't been found yet. Five-year-old Bobby had open-heart surgery when he was four years old and didn't walk or talk before that. Timmy lives with his grandmother because mom and dad don't want him. Terry also lives with grandparents after three years in foster care because of domestic violence in the home. Suddenly, it doesn't seem quite so unreasonable that these kids might occasionally rip up a paper in frustration or push a friend who takes their spot in line.

The behaviour is still unacceptable, but more understandable.

After two or more twelve-hour days of conferences in a row, yawning can become an issue. Understandably, parents can misinterpret this. I didn't have a yawning issue on the second day of conferences one year, because I was on my second cup of coffee by eight-thirty a.m. The result of that beverage choice, in that quantity, was that as I gestured wildly with my arms (as is my habit) while chatting with a calm and unsuspecting set of parents I sent that second extra large cup of coffee flying off the table to smash into pieces on the floor drenching a stack of textbooks.

The remaining eleven and a half hours of that day, the swampy carpet and drying books provided a comforting coffee shop smell and set the tone for some parental oversharing. So the new equation I learned that day was: an open coffee cup + an inability to talk without one's arms = fascinating revelations.

Potential hurdles to open communication abound. At one truly multicultural school in Australia we had quite a few parents that did not speak English very well. The most logical and often-used solution during parent/teacher interviews was translation by the student himself or an older sibling.

A problem arose one year when I was dishing out some rather unpleasant information about a child I shall call Leonard. Upon hearing the translation from Leonard's devoted big brother the parents smiled and nodded sweetly. At this point I was fairly sure that the happy little interpreter was not conveying the information in an entirely word-for-word manner. Some liberty was likely being taken with the content.

This is an occasion when you need to resort to some creative hand gestures. A fist punched into the palm of your other hand a couple of times in quick succession or a wringing of the neck action might do the trick. If all else fails, spit violently onto the report card, drop it and grind it into the floor with the heel of your shoe. If it is not displeasure you wish to communicate, perhaps you could mime sublime happiness and love while clutching the outstanding report card to your chest.

Other obstacles to free-flowing exchanges of information regarding student progress can come in the form of impatient younger siblings, cell phones, dissidence within the family itself and even pets.

Siblings get top billing in the aggravation category. Understandably these kiddos do not want to be there in the first place and the best way for them to speed up the process is to be as annoying as possible. I have had all my puzzles dumped out and the pieces mixed together, crayons eaten, all my books pulled out of bookshelves and papers gnawed on while the oblivious mommy sweetly sits in a tiny little student chair discussing the dubious virtues of the first edition of the hell-on-wheels wreaking havoc behind her.

One year during a student-led conference my well-rehearsed young student tried in vain to get her mom to look up from her cell phone for just a few seconds and pay attention to her presentation. I would have helped her out, but I was busy running interference on three younger siblings as they rampaged my room. These toddler terrors began by emptying my bookshelves, spreading the polished rocks in my rock jar all over the room and were in the process of watering the inside of my classroom mailbox with my adorable chameleon watering can when I 'refocused' them for the umpteenth time. Irritated, I turned to see that mommy was not only ignoring her little monsters, but still had not looked up from her cell phone to acknowledge her daughter's existence. Risking total destruction of my room I swooped in to point out a particularly cute story and drawing in her daughter's folder. Not even trying to disguise her texting, she glanced up in annoyance, murmured uh-huh and continued to text.

Cell phones have added a whole new dynamic to face-to-face teacher/parent meetings. I remember my grandmother (who was born in 1890) telling stories about how when automobiles were first on the roads there were no road rules yet and people drove wherever they liked. There was no right or wrong side of the road or speed restrictions. Road etiquette was up to personal interpretation. A similar situation exists now with mobile phones. People are being left to create their own standards of etiquette and the real live person sitting three feet away is not coming out on top. I have actually had parents reading texts while I am talking directly to them. I want to be snarky and say, "I am right here. I can see what you are doing."

Family discord can reach palpable levels of tension when divorced moms and dads attend conferences together. Since I take personal issue with doing double the number of conferences to accommodate adult human beings who can't be civil to each other for one half hour twice a year, I get to see some pretty ugly interactions.

The most intense conference in my career was the couple who came in and sat at opposite ends of my kidney shaped reading table with a good five feet of table top and four little chairs to keep them separated. They both sat slightly turned outwards so there was no chance of accidentally making eye contact with each other and they spoke only to me. Not once did they exchange a word with each other, yet one of them had the gall to question my judgment for marking their child with a relatively low score for 'Cooperates in groups'.

Pets attending conferences are rare, but I have had a few over the years. One year I had a big shaggy dog enter with the parents. Along for the ride were half a dozen children and apparently everybody else in the neighbourhood. The eighty-pound dog trotted straight over and lay down on my feet. Not at my feet, but ON my feet. Apparently this was a service dog, but no explanation was given to me at the time. All I got was slobbered on shoes.

Student-led conferences or learning journeys have become all the rage these days. In theory, this means that the student leads the parent through the learning process using learning activities and showcasing some of their better work. In reality this means a lot of preparation and coaching on the part of the teacher. Students need to be taught how to walk their parents through a math game, learning centre or how they edit their writing.

A strategy widely employed by teachers in the interest of self-preservation and job security is to develop a PowerPoint or use no-fail learning centres or computer games that the students have had extensive training in operating without a hitch. Everybody leaves feeling good about himself or herself. The teacher has proven that every kid can learn (or regurgitate as it may be), the student feels competent and the parents leave the room feeling proud.

However, if the whole exercise is truly authentic the teacher will spell out a few parameters in the days preceding this little endeavour and then toss the kid overboard to sink or swim. In this scenario, the parent will discover (in the spirit of true inquiry based learning of course) just exactly how well their child swims.

If Clueless Clementine is flailing at the side of the boat gulping gallons of water, sputtering about her stroke rate, grasping for the side of the boat and clearly in need of the life-ring held by the teacher, most parents conclude without much prompting that perhaps there are some very powerful reasons why she is not meeting the state standards just yet.

On the other hand, Excelling Emma gracefully glides alongside the boat with flawless technique, expounding meaningfully about how she practiced to reach this stage of perfection and waves off all attempts to assist her in any way. She has Olympic Gold in her sights and third grade is just the first exciting step. It is obvious to her parents that she has mastered all standards and they feel Emma surely could skip the next two grades. Now they want to know what you are going to do to extend their gifted genius.

Indifferent Ida takes apathy to new and dizzying heights and just rolls on her back and lets the boat pull away. When her parents call after her with questions about her personal learning journey she shrugs half-heartedly and points to the life-ring. When thrown the ring by the teacher she still remains adrift. At this point her parents are willing to admit that perhaps there are some motivation issues. Nothing the teacher could have said or any 'body of evidence' collected on this kid could be as effective as watching their child flounder first-hand.

If games are part of the rotation in the student-led scenario the competitive nature of parents and kids can come into play. In our first grade classroom we had several card and dice games we played to practice math facts. Some families became so competitive while playing *Go Fish for Tens* or *Top It* that I was pretty sure they had staked the family home or several million dollars on the game. They slapped the cards down yelling, "Ha!" or "Booya!" When granny got up, bounced the rubber dice off the floor while gyrating her hips and yelling, "Woo hoo!" I knew it was time to move on to looking at writing samples.

They say the apple doesn't fall far from the tree. Most veteran teachers will insist the attitude doesn't fall far from the tree in most cases. Now of course this attitude matching does not always ring true. As was the case with the darling well-behaved and studious child I spoke of earlier with the texting mom, some kids are incredibly resilient and find their own way in spite of less than perfect parents. Conversely some parents can be doing everything right and still end up with a challenging kid. I say challenging, because some of the most challenging little students end up being creative and inspiring adults. This is a possibility I like to dangle out there for desperate and exhausted parents to grasp onto. After all, it worked for me. Trust me, folks, my husband and I attended some interesting and mildly confronting conferences as our kids progressed through school and they are all now happy, productive and successful adults.

One of the most gratifying feelings for a teacher is when children actually pull off a student-led learning journey successfully. The vision goes like this: As parents come in they were greeted at the door by their little angels, who then smoothly and seamlessly walked them through a series of learning games, quality work samples, interactive inquiry boards, an art activity and a tough fitness circuit. Executed with enthusiasm, it is a thing of beauty and parents, students and their adoring teachers have a ball!

Dreams do come true.

Advice on conferences:

1. Take a sedative.
2. Insist on name tags.
3. Provide no life-rings.

Assemblies and School Concerts

An assembly is by definition a gathering. People assemble for rallies, political speeches, concerts, etc. Sometimes, as in legislative assemblies, it is expected that you attend if you are a member, but actually you just turn up if you want to. Schools and prisons are an exception. If the school assembly day is every other Friday then you and your class must be there. It is frowned upon and unacceptable to just say, "Nah, we don't feel like coming this week."

Assemblies serve many different purposes depending on the school. The only constant is that all schools have assemblies. Fortunately at the middle and high school levels these generally occur for special occasions, to bestow honours or for visiting presenters. At the primary school level they occur biweekly or monthly depending on the school. At most primary schools a class or grade level is featured or runs the assembly on a rotating basis. This is a chance for that class to share their learning, make a point, promote a cause or just entertain the rest of the school. Some teachers live for this opportunity. I do not.

Eager as most kids are to get out of class, most of the time assemblies are not at the top of their list of alternative activities. The biggest reason for this in my opinion is the seating arrangement. The best imagery I can come up with is a stockyard.

Minus the stink in most cases, the floor of the gym is like a stockyard. Kids are jammed up right next to each other, yet still expected to sit cross-legged. I relate best to the kids with Bambi legs, as that was my reality. Folding those lanky legs up under their chin to avoid taking up their neighbour's space results in balancing unsteadily on their pointy butt bones for an hour. When they unclasp their arms from around their legs in order to clap for a performance they lose their balance and their razor sharp elbows smack the kid next to them in the ear. Another whole set of issues comes from being too short to see over the kids in front or too fidgety to sit still.

Yet, we persevere. We all agreed wholeheartedly that the cultural experience of watching your fellow students dance awkwardly, sing out of tune, or fail to fluently read their own writing is of paramount importance to the academic achievement of the student body. The best performances of all (and most likely to inspire others) come from the school band.

I truly am amazed at how band directors can take a group of kids who can't even tap along to *Three Blind Mice* the first week of school and have them making an actual sound come out of a trumpet by the end of first term. This is exceptionally good stuff. However, why do we have to be along on this journey? Even kindergarteners who have been known to pretend they are impressed with my pathetic attempt at drawing a stick man, have no reservation at plugging their ears when the fledgling school band attempts something really tricky like *Twinkle Twinkle Little Star*.

Parents eat this stuff up though. They record it all on their cell phones for posterity. They save all the silly certificates in boxes in the attic forever. They heap praise on their little darling for earning a certificate that rewards them for sharpening their own pencil.

Most kids these days are accustomed to this over-affirmation from playing sports. Our oldest son realised the truth when he was a teenager and found a medal he had earned when he was eight. This big fancy gold medal was from *Little Athletics* and was engraved with *Most Improved.* He held it up and declared, "I am pretty sure this means that I really sucked at the beginning, doesn't it?" You got it son.

A standout runner I had the pleasure of coaching on a junior team when she was about seven years old received her end-of-the-year medal and turned it over to read the back. It said *Everybody is a Champion*! She ran her fingers over the engraving. Then she looked up at me shaking her head and emphatically stated, "Well that is just not true at all!"

Before we moved back to Australia I sorted through several boxes of certificates, ribbons, trophies and other awards bestowed on our four kids over the years. A fair few were legitimately earned during sporting events, but a significant portion were bogus certificates awarded for just doing what my generation did at school back in the day to keep from getting a smack. I phoned up the kids and not only did they not want the bogus stuff, but had sufficiently moved on from past glories to not even be interested in keeping any of the medals they earned for beating all the couch potatoes in the mile run at school.

Preparing a class of students for presenting at an assembly can eat up an enormous amount of class time in the weeks before the performance. By the time the kids perform they are thoroughly sick of the songs and neither they nor the teachers can get the tune out of their heads when they go to bed at night. The kids are actually hungry for new learning and say odd things like, "When are we going to have reading groups again?" Meanwhile the hoarse and weary teachers are hoping they catch a nasty virus before Friday.

Despite pressure from the anti-competition era in which we currently live, some schools still have the privilege of holding an annual talent show. The big difference is that no winner is declared. Kids just get up on stage and do what they believe they do well. Because we – both parents and teachers – are loath to tell a child they are not talented we have now been subjected to a surge in enthusiasm for showcasing dubious talent. In the age of reality TV, this is entertainment at its finest.

Who doesn't enjoy watching a group of rhythmically challenged, pimple faced, scrawny white boys stomp their way through a rap number? Likewise we are entranced by a group of uncoordinated, out of sync, out of tune pre-adolescent girls dressed in spangled outfits dancing and singing to a girly pop song. These performances are topped only by trying to unravel magic carried out with playing cards before our very eyes from nineteen rows back. Honestly though it truly is entertaining.

I say, "Bravo!" I shout a big yay to these risk taking kids and hope with all of my heart that they will have the good fortune of their parents accidentally deleting the recording of those fifteen seconds of fame.

The trumped up version of an assembly performance is a school concert. Most schools have a version of this extravaganza annually. Each class or grade level performs for the school body and parents on the stage, in costumes, after rehearsing for an absolute eternity. Preparations begin weeks before the scheduled performances. Students are steered by their teachers into 'choosing' a story to tell via songs or a play. The whole thing is even better if the performance can deliver some sort of moral or politically correct message in the process. Depending on the size of the school this could be one fabulous evening of entertainment or separated grade levels stretched over several evenings to accommodate the adoring crowds.

Having just spent the past couple of weeks prepping a group of kindergarteners for this year's school concert, the whole exhausting process is very fresh in my mind. We are currently coaching sixty-seven little future Oscar Award winners towards an original and creative version of Dr. Seuss's *The Lorax*. This involves asking five and six-year olds to listen, move, sing, dance, speak and generally follow multiple directions, in sequence, in synchronisation with others, without shouting, pushing, rolling on the floor, or otherwise behaving like children.

This requires a special skill set from teachers. We must be creative, clever, patient, flexible, firm, organised, nurturing, understanding, all-seeing and borderline insane. Strategies during rehearsal include prompting, prodding, rearranging, cajoling, bribing, threatening, and praising. All of these can (and sometimes do) happen within a span of thirty seconds and even simultaneously. Despite the anxiety, frustration, exasperation and potential trauma encountered during these productions the kids do learn the value of being part of something bigger than themselves. If they are really lucky their parents have it all recorded for posterity.

Assembly and concert survival tips:

1. Breathe deeply.
2. Take credit for nothing.

Meetings

Meetings are an unfortunate fact of life in most professions and it is no different for teachers. Most schools have a weekly staff meeting whether there is anything to talk about or not. I have taught in a couple of schools that meet only on an *as needed* basis, but they are few and far between.

Many meetings start with a mini pep rally. Most principals have attended corporate management seminars where they have learned to create a yearly theme, begin weekly meetings with celebrations and other positive motivational stuff. A 'celebration' can be anything from, 'Our choir made it into the District Competition' to 'Jason stayed in his own personal space for three whole minutes last week' or 'Jane didn't kick anybody in the shin at recess this week'.

I have seen the full spectrum of staff meeting arrangements. Some are casual affairs where teachers meet slouched in comfy chairs in the staff lounge with a cup of coffee pretending they're having a friendly little chat. Then there are the super formal meetings with printed agendas, assigned note takers and take-away work. Standard meeting formats lie somewhere in between. Teachers sit in somebody's classroom, loosely following an agenda and hashing over issues that are of concern to only a handful of participants at any one time.

The aspect that makes these gatherings bearable for me is my affinity for observing human reactions, interactions and public responses from my colleagues. Children are not the only ones with ADD, ADHD, a propensity for crying, anger issues, paranoia or a simple lack of common sense or respect.

Let's start with ADD and ADHD. From my own observations I can state with some authority that in a room of say forty people, there will be at least twenty displaying symptoms of either ADD or ADHD. I am not claiming all of these people have been diagnosed with either of these modern day maladies. Most likely for most of these overworked educators their actions are just a natural reaction to the circumstances they find themselves in. So as a result, at least ten are checking email, playing a game on their phone or writing sub plans for tomorrow. Another five are bouncing a leg or drumming their fingers on the table. The remaining five stare out the window or at the ceiling.

The disrespectful ones are chatting quietly with their neighbour. The paranoid ones are trying to figure out if a restrictive new mandate was caused by their actions. The angry ones are building to a verbal barrage as soon as the opportunity presents itself. Meanwhile over in the corner the crier is quietly wiping her eyes with a tissue. At one of my schools we had a lovely woman who got emotional over nearly everything. If we made it through an entire staff meeting without a tear shed by her we were not sure that the meeting had had any real substance at all.

Nothing beats adult circle time for production of tears. Every year at one of my schools we were given a lump of clay at the beginning of the year. Our principal's philosophy of teaching was that students were lumps of clay, which we as teachers shaped throughout the year. However she took that popular view a step further and maintained that the kids shaped us as well. The idea was that we would keep the lump of clay in our desk drawer and then sculpt it into a meaningful image of how our students had shaped us at some significant point during the year.

The reality was that a day or so before our end-of-year meetings we all scrambled to find that lump of clay and come up with an idea for our creation. This principal actually had done time in the trenches before becoming a principal. So being a realist, she always provided sculpting tools and more lumps of clay for those of us who had misplaced ours. She allowed us to sculpt during the daylong meetings. At the end of the two days we would stand in a circle with our clay creations and share. Talk about emotional! This was group therapy at its finest. Through laughter and tears we would share our experiences though our fledgling art pieces.

As a form of self-flagellation some of us weary souls take on roles on district level committees in the misguided assumption that we will somehow make a difference. It does make a difference, but to whom and how is the question I have been left wondering as I have sat on some of these committees for so long that the wheel is truly reinvented before my very eyes.

Most of my time teaching in Colorado I served as my school's representative on a committee that consisted of a panel of teachers who met once a month with the school district superintendent. The idea was that we brought questions and issues from our colleagues to this forum and the superintendent attempted answers or sidetracked us.

My longevity on these committees is due to just one factor. I call it ADHFD (Attention Deficit Hyper Focus Disorder). My ADHFD allows me to stray from that which most bores me and allows me to focus intently on that which has caught my eye and inspires me to give it more intense scrutiny. I have learned that the trick to getting people to read a report on issues relevant to their professional careers (but of no real interest to them) is to frontload or sprinkle the report with observations of human nature. Thanks to my ADHFD I am quite capable of noting and enhancing those observations.

One month I got to the meeting early. With my spare three minutes I had time to analyse my colleagues as they came in. Without any prior information a seasoned educator such as myself can pick the grade level and subject area with considerable accuracy. I started with the easy ones and described them in my notes. The sweat suit was a dead give away for PE. The be-spectacled fellow in the suit and tie was obviously a math teacher. Paint in the ear was clearly art. Tapping the table was most likely music. Gaining confidence, I went on to describe the other people in the room.

I moved on to describing the more subtle clues garnered from the scattering of women in the room when I arrived. One had to be a high school language arts teacher. She was frantically marking a massive pile of handwritten papers and looked up every so often to babble random things to the woman next to her. The woman next to her had the glazed over look of a fellow high school teacher who had seen and heard similar random things all day long.

Another dishevelled woman sat and stared at the wall, apparently the victim of total exhaustion. She was obviously a thirty-year vet of first grade. Trying in vain to engage the catatonic one in conversation was a woman who referred to herself as 'we', thus giving herself away as a kindergarten teacher. The wild-eyed, twitchy ones are dead giveaways as middle school teachers. The subject taught in that case is irrelevant.

I was able to peg the woman that I eventually plunked down next to as a special education teacher as soon as she reached over and moved my full cup of tea away from the edge of the table. I know she also wanted to tuck my napkin in at my neck the first time I dripped the aforementioned tea on my sweatshirt. She resisted.

Advice on surviving irrelevant meetings:

1. Just relax and relish the fact that nobody is currently asking you to actually do anything but listen.
2. Use the time to study human nature.
3. Learn to sleep with your eyes open.

Recess – AKA the Jungle

There is a certain numbing factor that evolves over time when one is exposed to a constant stream of senseless over-stimulation. Recess is one such ongoing assault to normal sensibilities. A favourite part of the day for most kids, recess has been a part of institutionalized education from the raw beginnings.

Crazy Craig, a short wiry kindergarten boy in Colorado, embodied the spirit of recess like no other children I have ever known before or since. He would emerge from the classroom door, blink a couple of times in the bright sunlight and plant his stubby little feet for a second with his hands on his hips as he glanced from side to side and then begin to run.

Crazy-eyed and determined, he would just run. He ran with the lateral movements of an NFL football player keeping his base wide for balance. With the quick feet of a boxer he was at the ready for quick changes of direction. His eyes were always wide open with a startled stimulant-induced look about them. His arms were tense and flexed with elbows out for added stabilisation as he zoomed in and out among his compatriots exuding enthusiasm for freedom, for the outdoors, and for life! He would eventually slow a bit and even pause briefly to express admiration for a schoolmate's sport prowess, sand construction, mud dam, or jungle gym contortion, but he never, ever stopped. Never. Not until the whistle blew to line up to go back inside.

Injury is frequently the inevitable result when dozens of children are running about all willy-nilly on unyielding concrete surfaces at recess. Not all children have the zig and zag down like Crazy Craig. A child streaming blood from all four limbs often fails to evoke any emotional response from the ever-vigilant teachers on duty when it is approximately the two thousand four hundred and forty-fifth time they have seen the same trauma.

My standard procedure is to take a crumpled tissue from my pocket (clean and unused of course) and hand it to the whimpering child with instructions to wipe up the drips. If necessary I contact the office on my walkie-talkie, tell them a walking wounded is on his way and then admonish the child to perhaps tie his shoes next time, then give him a hug.

If the child needs additional comforting words, I resort to my mother's famous quote. When we were sufficiently injured as children to attempt to garner sympathy through a display of tears she would soothe us with, "Don't worry. It'll feel better when it stops hurting." Since I was usually too distracted by watching blood ooze through those tiny holes in the Band-Aid to fully take in her words, it was only when I got much older that I realised this advice was a bunch of BS.

Daily bloody carnage is the direct result of the maniacal behaviour generated the moment kids reach the playground. The majority of the little ones run senselessly about the grounds for at least the first five minutes with no real purpose or objective. That is OK. I condone this action wholeheartedly, because the energy release is necessary if there is to be any semblance of calm when we return to the classroom.

The relatively sane individuals try, mostly to no avail to organise their deranged classmates into some sort of structured play. Soon these type As find each other, designate roles, such as princess, knight and unicorn and begin scripted role-play orchestrated by the future head cheerleader.

Older kids often will organise themselves into sport teams or walk about in clumps discussing the weighty issues of the world, like why they can't have Twinkies for lunch. They are the cool ones and they know it.

The uncool wander the fringes drifting in and out of other kids' games. Sometimes if the younger cool kids are engaged in some sort of fantasy play they are not even aware that the uncool have graced them with their presence until a particular role is missing. "Hey, where did that rock go that was just here a second ago? Hey you! Yeah you. Wanna play?" Stoked to be included, the rookie happily takes on the role of rock #3 until the unicorn sits on her.

In reality the uncool are often super cool and nobody recognizes it yet. As the phoenix flies by or the archaeologist brings you yet another dinosaur bone to examine, you realise that the world would be a pretty dull place if everybody played the princess game or felt obligated to play soccer just to fit in. Who would notice that the clouds looked like a dragon just now, or that the playground is covered in diamonds that just haven't been polished yet, or that the black dog that just galloped by is actually Sirius Black?

In addition to the constant escort often provided by some of the social misfits who tag alongside there is entertainment galore for the teacher on duty. Sometimes you watch as a child attempts a feat of physical prowess that you are fairly certain that particular child is not yet capable of executing with finesse and you mutter under your breath, "This can only end in tears." Nine times out of ten, it does.

For instance, one afternoon I watched a young boy attempt to stand on his hands. The trouble with this idea was two-fold. First, this young lad had arms about the diameter of spaghetti noodles and with as much strength. Second, his choice of surface for this trick was the concrete. To my astonishment, he actually managed to do a perfect handstand... for about one second. Then in slow motion, his left arm quivered for a second and then collapsed. Gravity took over at this point and his face made abrupt and rather uncomfortable contact with the concrete. As I rushed to scoop him up he rolled over, looked up at the sky, rubbed the blood off his left cheek with his sleeve and whispered, "Ouch."

Getting injured in action at playtime was much easier when I was a kid. Back in the day when parents were aware that life held some inherent risk and had not yet demanded the removal of all fun equipment, kids were gravely injured everyday on playground equipment designed to keep the population explosion in check. If anyone had bothered to do the research I am sure they would have found a direct correlation between the level of fun and the risk of injury.

Let's have a look at the big three in the maiming and fatality category back in the 60s. These would be the teeter-totter, the merry-go-round and the swings. If you are lucky you may still find some of these relics around in neglected neighbourhood parks, but you will not find them in school playgrounds any more. Here is why.

The teeter-totters (also called see-saws) that we played on at my elementary school growing up were about twelve to fifteen feet long and made of splintery wood painted green. They had a slight indent for your legs on an otherwise straight thick board attached to a pivot about three feet high. If you and your playmate were not of equal weight, which was always the case with me because I was a skinny little featherweight, the heavier kids had a distinct advantage in controlling the activity. There were several evil ways that the heavier kids could dislodge or launch a kid like me.

The simplest way was to come down hard and fast so that when the heavy end hit the ground the stick insect (me) was bounced off her perch at the top. If you hung on tight (which I usually did) your butt would fly off the seat, legs flail about a bit, but you may just stay on for more abuse.

A more nerve-racking technique was to hold flyweight up the top and tease her till she begged to be let down. As soon as the pleading one made it clear she wanted down NOW the big guy would simply get off, leaving the other end (again me) to plummet back to earth at high speed. Why in the hell I repeatedly agreed to play on the teeter-totters is beyond me.

When not being tortured by bigger classmates (these days we would call it bullying – even though I chose to repeatedly get back on that crazy contraption) we used the teeter-totter to run back and forth on. You would start at one end and run or walk upwards towards the centre pivot. As you reached the pivot point you had to keep your balance as the board tilted the other way and you ran down the other side.

The challenge here, of course, was to be the fastest. My equally scrawny siblings and me used to practice these techniques after hours and over vacations when our classmates weren't around in hopes of this activity becoming the preferred teeter-totter game at which we could then excel. Like many best laid plans we did not have the political clout despite our numbers to change the recess culture at our school.

Merry-go-rounds have all but disappeared from most public parks and school playgrounds. These centrifuges-of-death came in both wood and metal versions. Kids piled on this deadly disc and hung on while other kids grabbed onto the handles or edges and spun the darn thing around as fast as possible. Nauseous children clung to the spinning vessel trying not to spew up their recently ingested lunch.

To my delight when my own children were young, there was still a merry-go-round in the park reserve across the road from our house. My little daredevils took this entertainment to a whole new nerve shattering level by getting the stupid thing up to speed and then dangling from the metal side bars by one arm so that their entire bodies were flying horizontal to the ground. An added challenge was to avoid the family dog trying to grab a leg as it flew past. The dog-dodging element ended abruptly one day when the frisky canine got inadvertently kicked in the jaw. Yelping and whining, he dashed home to lick his wounds and no longer participated in the game.

Swings can still be found on public playgrounds, but not at schools any more. In addition to clueless kids walking under them and getting clocked by the kids on the swings, there was the issue of inherently dangerous trapeze inspired tricks upping the injury count. Trapeze dismounts were best accomplished on those really tall swings with a full-swing arc long enough for a whole class of kids to wander underneath.

A favourite in my neighbourhood growing up and later with my own youngest son was the circus flip. First you had to get the swing going really high – high enough to get that bump effect when the chains slacken just a bit near the top. I'm talking about the kind of high that leads you to believe that you could actually twirl right over the top pole. Once you reach that height where your stomach drops just as the swing begins to descend you are high enough to attempt the flip. Just before the top of the forward swing you jump off, executing a back flip in the air before hopefully landing on your feet. I am sorry to report that, unlike my nimble son, I never successfully executed this move. Not once.

The chief issue with swings at school was not so much the people on the swings and their crazy tricks, but the oblivious humans who wandered into the path of the swingers only to get flattened or hit multiple times before the swinger could stop. Some swings were designed of materials and shapes that lent themselves to more lethal injury than a barefoot heel, rubber toed shoe or youngster's backside could deliver. In particular animal-shaped swings made of metal come to mind.

One day at the lakeside park near my parents' house my husband and I were leisurely relaxing on the grass some distance from the playground and somewhat inattentively watching our four young children play. As we absent-mindedly watched the playground activity, we saw a distracted toddler wander in front a steel stallion meant to be a kiddie swing with a two-hundred-pound eight-year-old astride its back. The shiny metal mane of the bucking bronco rammed the clueless kiddo in the temple and sent her flying. Whoa! Mouths agape, we both marvelled at the resilience of the plucky pint-sized victim as she picked herself up off the ground, dusted off her knees and shook the sand out of her hair before deciding this was a situation worthy of tears.

It was only when she began to wail, clench her tiny fists and go after the would-be knight on his bloodied steed, that we realised the enraged ramming victim was our darling daughter. As we held the icepack provided by the lifeguards to the enormous purple horn growing out the side of her head we admonished ourselves for not watching her closer.

At no point did it even cross our minds to sue the eight-year-old or his parents, or the county park department, or the offending horse. We did not demand the removal of all swings from the park, the state, or the western hemisphere. We did, however, embark on a little belated education for our little one and her siblings on spatial awareness. We also moved our viewing point a little closer on future visits.

Grateful that there was at least sand under the swings the day our youngest daughter took the blow to the head (which I will admit was not the first or the last of her childhood), my husband and I recalled that *back in our day* there were no cushy rubberized surfaces to bounce off of. All of the scary equipment, along with an assortment of climbing bars, tetherballs and balance beams were usually installed over asphalt. A broken limb, chipped tooth, fractured skull or stitches were pretty much a right of passage back in the day. Nobody sued the school or tried to find out who the evil one was that hurt their child on purpose. Our parents simply came and got us, took us to the doctor to get stitched up and sent us limping back to school the next day. We all walked around with skinned knees, lumps on our foreheads and a healthy sense of our physical limitations.

My childhood elementary school in Minnesota even upped the ante and provided opportunities to challenge our physical prowess by flooding a portion of the staff parking lot in the winter so we could ice-skate at recess. I spent a great deal of the winter every year with sprained wrists.

These days not only is the playground equipment limited to items with no moving parts and a safety surface softer than a pillow-top mattress, but the playground comes with a whole set of detailed rules. We actually take the kids out several times a year and instruct them as to how they should use each piece of equipment and why that rule is important. No more launching classmates into near earth orbit from a teeter-totter, no sliding down the slide head first with a pile of friends on top or in a human train and for heaven's sake never, ever, ever climb a tree!

In my opinion, recess is more than just an energy release and a place for some of the laws of the jungle to play out. It is also the birth of social status and manoeuvring. As teachers we would like to think that social development takes place under our careful guidance in the classroom. Not so. The social hierarchy and the construction of meaningful world relations have their roots in school playgrounds all over the world.

From the moment a toddler gains his feet and wobbles over to a creature smaller and wobblier than him he has a decision to make. Does he smile, caress and help stabilize that weaker creature or does he push it down. The child's first gut reaction does not determine which course this child will take throughout life. More important is his reaction to what he has done. Was there regret and empathy after the push or satisfaction? Did he have a warm fuzzy feeling and a sense of pride or was he less than enthralled with his performance when he showed his softer side?

Regardless of where a child's social development is at by the time she reaches primary school there is much to be learned on the playground about how the politics works. The social web is tricky and negotiation skills are a priority. This is the venue where future leaders learn how to rebrand themselves. At the primary school age this has very little to do with clothing, especially if the school requires a uniform, although this is still possible. Our youngest daughter (the feisty one) always wore mismatched socks as a way to assert her independence against her public school uniform in Australia. Because social statements are rarely made with clothing at this level, most often status must be achieved through behaviour.

Of course, the Feisty One did not really need to distinguish herself in this way, because despite her small stature she wielded an enormous amount of clout. She was a fearless champion of justice. Legend has it that at recess one dark and stormy day Rude Rodney was bullying Chubby Chuck (our back fence neighbour) for his substantial bulk. When a playmate rushed over to the Feisty One to report this injustice she sprang into action.

With her feet planted firmly at the cusp of the playground hill and her hands on her hips Feisty One bellowed, "RODNEY!" Rodney and everybody else on the playground froze in their tracks. As the story was recounted to me, what ensued was 'like the parting of the Red Sea.' The student body collectively moved aside as Feisty One marched down the hill and punched Rodney in the stomach, since that was as high as she could reach. Nobody reported the incident to school authorities and Rodney never bullied Chubby Chuck again. Social justice at its finest.

On the surface, playground sports seem like the best and most wholesome activity for students to engage in. Unfortunately fuelled by the poor behaviour and argumentative attitudes of our overpaid TV sporting heroes, playground soccer can gain the intensity of the World Cup. As recess time approaches, the boys pull up their socks, glance knowingly and give a slight nod of approval to potential teammates and nervously adjust their underwear in anticipation of the bell. When dismissed they dash out the door to enthusiastically pound and pummel each other for an exhilarating half an hour.

The ensuing injuries and blood are carefully concealed until the return bell sounds so as not to lose playing time. All of the injustices are revealed as the muddy and dishevelled athletes return to the classroom. If the walking wounded are to be believed, the carnage was worthy of a full-scale forensic investigation. Resist the urge to sort it out. Playing blind referee after the fact is a worse mistake than tossing a bit of fish to a seagull.

A child who realises he is beginning to be seen as a bully can cast a new light on his behaviours. He realises one day how his behaviour looks to others and he justifies himself with, "I just took the ball from him, because I was going to show him how to kick it right, so he won't be embarrassed." This young man will one day convince his employees that reducing their benefits is the way to go, because it improves the cash flow, which in turn will allow improvements to the image of the company, which of course will naturally be good for all.

Likewise the future Secretary of State is honing her skills by applying sanctions within her friendship groups. "I will only include Sophie in our game if she gives me her fruit rollups every day for the next month." The group sees this as perfectly acceptable, because they know if they don't agree with her then S of S will withhold her own limited supply of Fritos from the group. All dissidents who do not agree with the new policy also potentially risk personal sanctions or possible expulsion from the coalition.

Of course the level and intensity of all of this business and political training ramps up in middle school and high school. Here social standing and political clout are way more important than academic standing. Those who feel no need to become involved in the status wrangling either choose a close-knit (think small town) comfortable cluster to hang out with, become a lone wolf, or concentrate all of their energy into high achievement in academics and/or sports. The strength of character developed in the mini jungle that is the school playground sets the stage for which route a student may take down the road.

Back in my day, when playgrounds still had some challenging physical activities with all their inherent risks, there was far less need to buy into the political system. Deprived of natural adrenaline producing activity these days, kids sometimes feel the need to resort to covert operations to get the occasional thrill. Shenanigans do happen, even under the eagle eyes of the teachers who have all been specifically trained in detecting concealed weapons and mal-intent. The following chapter gives a sampling of the sort of mischief that can occasionally border on petty crime.

Recess advice:

1. Never, ever turn your back.
2. Carry tissues and band-aids.
3. Enjoy the show.

Criminal Activity

Over the years I have been witness to some petty crime within the confines of school property. In my experience most of these transgressions have been in the genre of theft and vandalism, but occasionally seep into the realm of physical violence. Seeing as children are miniature humans and felons were once children, it is not surprising that some children engage in somewhat errant behaviours. Considering the immaturity of a child's basic locus of control it is also not surprising how comically inept kids can be at deception and evasive action.

Vandalism in the form of graffiti at the elementary school age is far less creative than one would think. Having (at the tender age of six) scraped my own name into the cinder block walls of my basement along with my seven and a half year old brother, I can't really criticise this form of artistic expression. I also can't recall the logic that drove me and my brother to slide a small desk in front of our signatures. We apparently held a misguided belief that nobody would ever find them. But I can tell you that fifty-odd years later this same logic is alive and well with the younger generation.

One fine spring day three of my first grade students wrote their names big and bold with permanent markers on the outside wall of the school in broad daylight at recess with several dozen other students and a couple of teachers right there. When their signatures were discovered on the wall they denied it to the ends of the earth. They obviously had not thought it through. If they were going to brazenly deface the wall of their own school in broad daylight they could at least stand a fighting chance of not being accused if they did not sign their names to the work.

When inevitably tattled on by their ever-loyal classmates the three vandals denied it in unity. When the lunchtime playground monitor tried to get a confession they closed ranks and refused to fess up. So, the problem returned to the classroom for my final judgment.

Unable and unwilling to sort this all out during class-time, I sent the darlings to the office to let our commanding officer unravel the mystery. When the principal came back to the class with these three pretty little liars in tow she asked the class if they had any clues that might help solve the case. Tiring of the whole sordid affair, one grave-faced and sincere young lad put up his hand to volunteer his information. "It was spirits. I saw them. Spirits did it."

Taken off guard by this declaration the bemused principal mumbled, "Wh… what?"

Looking her in the eyes and leaning in closer he repeated slowly, "Spirits did it. White spirits."

Nodding her acknowledgement of this suggestion and desperately trying to conceal her mirth she turned back to the class and told everyone they needed to go home and ponder this situation and come back tomorrow with either a confession or information on how these names came to be on the wall.

The next day all three girls fessed up. When they were in the office waiting while the principal wrote up the offence they held hands and prayed for strength, which was a new twist for this principal. She popped by later in the morning to whisper to me, "You will be pleased to know that it was not, in fact, white spirits who wrote on the wall." Well, thank heavens for that. White spirits are tricky to catch.

Thieves under the age of ten are also not very sneaky. They take things that will be missed. They take things that have somebody else's name engraved on them. They take things that don't fit into their pockets or backpacks. They take things that they don't even need or want. Of course sometimes you get a kid who really has a strong affinity for the skill and then you get the birth of a career thief. I had one such kleptomaniac in my class one year.

She started out with a bang. She stole a pair of purple cowgirl boots bedecked with distinctive bling, which had been shared for Show and Tell just that morning. I am not sure where she thought she would be able to wear them. When confronted by her mother that afternoon at home (when her mother found the boots in her backpack) she told Mommy that she had earned them as a prize from Mrs. Davis' treasure box. I did have one very impressive treasure box, but I was not in the habit of stocking it with cowgirl boots. Sensing this might be the case, Mama didn't buy the story and dragged her darling daughter into school with the contraband to confess.

Now I would love to tell you that this swift action by Mama cured my little sticky fingers of her kleptomania, but it was not to be so. The following day she stole the same classmate's gym shoes and tucked them into somebody else's backpack for some perverse reason.

This was rapidly followed the next day by lifting lip-gloss from the same victim's desk. As usual she denied this, but after a tip off from a classmate that the lip-gloss was right there in the thief's back pocket I made her empty her pockets. Lo and behold, there it was. As she withdrew it from her pocket she feigned surprise and gasped, "How did that get there?"

Bursting into tears as I marched her to the office, she begged unsuccessfully for mercy and insisted that her dad had warned her that if she continued down this path she would end up in 'kid jail'. Really, honey? Maybe you should have listened, seeing as daddy dished that advice out from behind bars.

Not all juvenile offenders are as chronic as my little second-generation felon. Most are one-timers. They try it out, are no good at it and give it up. I am happy to report that this child, after three miserable failures eventually decided this was not to be her vocation and she gave it up.

Lunches and snacks are a popular target of fledgling thieves, mainly because the evidence can be consumed and it becomes very hard to prove that the thief is in possession of the contraband. Unfortunately for the kids, being tidy eaters is not a common characteristic of youngsters. When a child has hastily gobbled a cupcake in the hallway it is highly likely that she has some sticky evidence plastered to her face when she comes back from a supposed trip to the toilet. Despite the proximity to other humans when on the hunt these little scavengers still manage to satisfy their hunger without depleting their own resources.

If the backpack hooks are outdoors, as they are in the majority of the Australian schools I have taught in, it can be trickier to read the clues. My class one year was becoming more stressed and disturbed each day as tasty treats went missing from their backpacks with increasing frequency. Accusations were flying and kids were beginning to keep a wary eye on each other at all times. Yet the heists continued. The classroom had floor to ceiling windows the length of the outside wall. It was baffling how somebody was getting away with this daily.

One day I was gone for the morning and when I returned the relief teacher warned me that he had seen a scruffy little dog poking around near the backpacks. Interesting. As expected, at lunchtime a couple of sandwiches were missing. Suspecting our canine friend, I explained the situation to the distraught kids and with my best told-you-so face on I reminded them once again to keep their backpacks zipped and up on the hooks. Since Fido was only a little pup and did not have thumbs, the thievery ended.

Special pencils, small toys and scented markers are other easy marks. For the most part the younger the child the less likely they are to have a good plan in place once they have lifted something from a classmate. I have found many a stolen item stuffed in the offender's desk or cubby. They may often blatantly use the item even as the distraught former owner is making a claim that it belongs to them. The child in possession of the goods, who now adheres to the *possession is nine tenths of the law* theory, may admit to having seen this particular pencil with Kalamazoo engraved on it in the hand of the accuser earlier in the day. However, he also stubbornly claims that his grandpa bought him the same pencil when he (coincidentally) was also in Kalamazoo, Michigan last week. It doesn't take Sherlock to solve that one.

At one point we had an epidemic of what our staff dubbed *sticker fraud* at our school. As the keystone to our PBIS (Positive Behaviour Intervention System) we give out shiny little star stickers whenever we caught kids doing the right thing. When a child filled a card (about twenty-five stars) she could turn it in on designated days in the lunchroom for prizes. As they moved through the rainbow colours of the cards the prizes got bigger. Back in my day we called that bribery, but calling it positive reinforcement works for me.

Anyhow, we discovered that some of our little darlings were peeling stickers off other kids' cards and putting them on their own. Like the beaver activity mentioned earlier, this was very hard to detect. Most of us kept the cards in a pocket chart somewhere in the room so the old switcheroo was not difficult to make. Removal of the offending hand is not an option in our culture so we opted for taking the entire card away from offenders when fraud was discovered and moving them back one card in the series.

Some students – like my cowboy boots thief – are compelled to follow the *go big or go home* credo and don't bother with stickers or pencils, but keep their eye out for bigger fish. No better place exists for these opportunities than at the middle school level. At this age some kids have cell phones, iPads, and other enticing technology and others do not. Flaunting these items often results in losing these items. The year that I taught middle school I saw some very brazen theft attempts right in my classroom, but a successful larceny was never achieved. To avoid investigative duties I told the students and e-mailed parents that I would not be wasting learning time sorting out disagreements over stolen property.

Secondary school shenanigans often have more dangerous repercussions. Our oldest daughter had her long hair set on fire while waiting in line at the school cafeteria window when she was about thirteen years old. Quick thinking classmates snuffed it out with minimal scorching, but naturally she was a bit disturbed by this event. Knowing the limited mental reasoning ability of her cigarette lighter wielding classmate we were not interested in holding the school responsible for this particular kid's actions.

The next morning my husband took the smoke alarm off the ceiling and hung it on the back of our daughter's shirt as she was getting ready to leave for school. She was not particularly amused. As she removed the alarm from her back, the phone rang. It was her paternal grandma asking to speak to the little fire torch. Expecting more gratifying sympathy than she had received from her family thus far, she took the call. After speaking to her grandmother she smiled grudgingly, handed the phone back to me and hustled off to school. Apparently her darling grandmother had begun sweetly singing, "You light up my life…"

Our oldest son came to grief at the same school through similar peer stupidity. Somebody had loosened the front wheel of his bicycle while it was parked in the school bike compound. Unbeknownst to our trusting son this had become a popular 'joke' at the school.

When he bumped off the curb and the front wheel popped off he took a dive over the handlebars.

Several hours in the ER was all it took to bring his rattled brain back around, but he needed a new helmet. Later we found out several other wheels had been loose that week, but since those kids weren't trying to jump curbs they didn't end up concussed. Nobody ever took responsibility for the bicycle adaptations, but thankfully once word of the unfortunate consequences got out the shenanigans stopped.

At the primary level it is all so much more concrete. Most of the time you see it happen. The kid says, "I didn't do it."

You reply, "I saw you."

They crack. They cry. My husband, who was not the best-behaved kid in school and often accused of various transgressions in his primary years (frequently with good reason) likes to tell a story about being falsely accused.

My husband-to-be and another young suspect were being dragged by their ears to the headmaster's office across the street amid threats of all sorts of dire consequences. Suddenly the other boy crumpled to his knees and sobbed out a confession right then and there in the middle of the street. This is the most common outcome of investigations in the primary years.

Physical violence of course is never tolerated. This is the reason that it must be a covert operation. Nobody wants to get caught with his fist in somebody else's eye.

Denial is the natural reaction to this type of accusation, but not all kids feel the need to deny. Certain kids in my class every year have no problem with fessing up to their transgressions. When I ask, "Did you hit Suzy?" the violent one replies, "Yup. She made me mad."

When I was a kid growing up in a family of eight my mother decided a cuss jar may help my siblings and I to think before swearing or retaliating against some perceived injustice with a slug. The deal was: if you swore you had to drop a penny in the jar, but if you hit or kicked a sibling you had to drop five cents into the jar. Just before Christmas the proceeds of the jar would be split eight ways. So, if you didn't pay in much over the course of the year you would make a profit. We kids thought this might work out well for us since our parents had a much richer vocabulary than any of us.

However, the violence clause was our downfall because some of us, in particular my brothers, deemed it well worth twenty-five cents to get in a solid five punches to appease a grudge. Similarly for some students, a trip to the principal's office is worth it to make a point with a classmate in a very physical and memorable way.

Advice on criminal investigations:
1. Patience.
2. Disguise any amusement.
3. Do not expect miracles of repentance.

The Meltdown

We've all seen it in grocery stores, in relatives' homes, on buses, in doctors' offices and anywhere else a child perceives an injustice may have occurred. A primary school aged child who throws herself on the floor wailing and flailing her arms about like a three-year-old has generally found success with this technique at home and feels confident in employing this strategy out in the bigger world. Anyone who has witnessed one of these full-blown tempests will assure you that the energy expenditure for one of these performances would not be worth the effort if the child did not fully expect to get what she wants at the end of the tirade. Nowhere is a child more likely to be asked to do something she doesn't want to do than in the classroom.

The classic full-blown tantrum or meltdown can be hard to predict sometimes, but the majority of the time any teacher with more than a few days of experience with a touchy child can see the signs of the approaching storm and head it off. However, the little darlings that have found greatest success with dramatic reactions at home are not easily dissuaded from this course of action. The trigger is often so tiny that the reaction seems akin to spontaneous combustion.

Meltdowns range from mild loss of composure to complete physical breakdown. My favourite tantrum to date (and the most baffling) was over a potato. I took away a little guy's potato. Now, I am not talking about the potato chips this child was about to eat for lunch. I am talking about a slightly soft, skin-on, raw potato that this child had brought along to school that morning. In an effort to be open-minded and fair I let the little guy 'share' about his potato and how it was indeed an earth material befitting of our current unit of inquiry in science.

We shall call our little scientist Spud. As Spud was about to shove the aged potato back into his hooded sweatshirt pocket I told him that the potato would need to reside in his backpack for the remainder of the day. He nodded and dutifully walked out to his hallway hook to put the potato in his backpack.

One might argue that my lack of follow-through caused the altercation that followed later that morning. We were in the library for our weekly lesson and book checkout when the potato rolled to a stop at my feet. Funny. I don't recall ever dodging potatoes in the library before.

Before I could reach down and retrieve the potato, Spud materialized from behind a book stack and grabbed it and shoved it back into his hoodie pocket. When I told Spud he would have to give me the potato for safe keeping until the end of the day you would have thought I had just shot his dog.

Spud collapsed like a rag doll on the floor and began to keen like a veiled woman at a funeral. He was inconsolable. Exasperated, I personally made no attempt to console him. However, seven-year-old girls can't resist circling around and rubbing the back of any creature that is in despair. Gathered up by the empathetic ones, Spud stumbled on out of the library with the rest of the class and straight into the path of the principal and deputy principal who were heading in our direction to see what tragedy had befallen a student so suddenly in the library. I informed them that I had caused the ruckus by 'taking his potato'. If this brief explanation confused them, they did not let on and just removed Spud from the scene.

The volume and endurance of some young tantrum experts is truly impressive. One such master of the art could hold a note longer than the most accomplished opera singer and still be heard above the sound of Air Force jets flying overhead. The source of his displeasure was always a bit of a mystery because he was so consistently miserable that discerning a defining moment that might have triggered the latest outburst was next to impossible.

Fortunately for me, this child was not in my class. One day he followed me around the playground during recess happily consuming a cupcake. I encouraged him to go run and play when he had finished, but he smiled (a rare treat) and continued to shadow me. As soon as I blew the whistle to signal the end of recess he threw himself on the ground and began to bellow. Inquiring as to what was the matter with him *now* I gently eased him to his feet. Throwing his head back to gain strength and volume he wailed, "I didn't get a chance to play!"

The quiet meltdowns are less disruptive for the class, but still just as challenging for the teacher who is charged with furthering this child's education. Little Timmy Tantrum, who is pouting under a table, is not marching along towards his full year of academic growth. Time under the table also has left him a couple of years short of expected social growth too.

Meltdowns are not reserved for the little ones. Middle school and high schools abound with catalysts for a meltdown. These meltdowns look a little different. Most often the full body is not involved, but the ripple effect can grind a lesson to a premature halt. When the Queen Bee is shooting eye daggers at her ex and texting (the modern day version of note passing) her dissatisfaction to her cadre of unwilling followers, the algebra lesson loses what tentative hold it had on the adolescent focus in the room.

The older the student gets the more likely the loss of composure is to involve swearing, name calling, door slamming or dramatic exits or entrances. Middle years kids begin to dabble in these. Though not as toxic as a high school meltdowns or as physically involved as a primary student, the drama of a ten-year-old's crisis can be just as exhausting for all parties. Most amusing are those that create their own embarrassment.

Gregory Grenade blew up one day and tossed his pencil case across the room. Startled and dismayed as his beloved case shattered and the shrapnel scattered across the floor, he scrambled over and began scooping up his belongings as his classmates stared in disbelief at such a display of anger. As he stomped his way back to his seat trying to juggle all of his pencils, markers and the splinters of plastic that once were his pencil case, his ever patient seatmate smoothed out the test he had crumbled in a ball and placed it carefully back on his desk. GG dropped his head unto the test still clutching the remains of his shattered belongings. Conveniently he had created his own consequences.

My advice on the subject of meltdowns:

1. Don't flatter yourself; it most likely had nothing to do with you.
2. Avoiding a meltdown can be a fruitless endeavor if you don't know the trigger.
3. Earplugs.

Classroom Management

Without proper classroom management... bad stuff happens. Despite a plethora of 'expert' advice on managing challenging behaviours there is no classroom management plan that can anticipate all possible student reactions, responses, impulses and actions.

Possible management enhancing tools include: bells, clapper sticks, rain sticks, tambourines, clapping hands, clicking fingers, or flicking lights. Here is the beauty of these tools. If all else fails most of these (except the light switch) can be used to smack the child. Joke, people! We all know that ever since the 70s it has been illegal to smack children at school. Although in 1995 my youngest son's kindergarten teacher was in her last year before retiring and didn't really care what anybody thought. She smacked kids on the bottom when they misbehaved. So they didn't.

An old education instructor of mine (we shall call him Ed) told a story of a time when he was being observed by his principal during his first year of teaching. Ed was teaching PE and as the kids entered the gym the class troublemaker swaggered in donning a backward baseball cap and a skull emblazoned black T-shirt with the sleeves ripped off. His bad attitude blew in with him like a billowing storm cloud. Wanting to circumvent any bad behaviour before it began, Ed casually strolled over and privately whispered some words to the young hoodlum. This gangster turned angel attracted the observing principal's attention and when the class was over he asked Ed what in the world he had said to the boy to get such a dramatic turnaround. Ed admitted he had used his own unorthodox method. He had told the boy, "One wrong move and I will rip your arms off, just like your sleeves." Ed did not advocate this classroom management technique in our current era of positive behaviour management. I think he was just still a little bit proud of himself.

Most of my generation who grew up with smacking, ear tugs, writing 'I will not talk', on the board a hundred times and other time honoured disciplinary measures would agree that the banning of physical punishment is a good thing. However, the ineffectiveness of modern measures can sometimes be frustrating.

No matter how engaging we are as teachers there are going to be some students who are just not buying it and will need some behaviour modification. Most schools these days adopt a school wide behaviour plan. These invariably are based on positive behaviour modification methods of some sort. This means we look for and reward good behaviour as opposed to punishing bad behaviours.

So, that leaves us with some choices when it comes to those kids who have a very limited experience with good behaviours. We can stage and then guide a kid into a good behaviour and then very quickly reward it before he messes it up. We can redirect a bad behaviour and steer the child into the correct behaviour, then reward instantly. Or we can lavish praise and rewards on those who show model behaviour all the time in hopes that the little monsters in the class see and want a piece of it. Naturally they will then flawlessly alter their own behaviour. This is all good in theory, but only touches the surface when it comes to those kids for whom boundary pushing is a way of life.

I once worked with a teacher who took on the persona of several different characters in his teaching. Schizophrenic perhaps? Maybe, but his method was effective. His characters each had a role to play in his classroom. You met him a few chapters back as Pirate Pete. One character was the storyteller, another the comforter, another disciplinarian, etc. I am not sure which role the pirate played, but one day when we were in a staff meeting this teacher was still carrying his pirate sword. This was back in the day when adults could still distinguish between a weapon and a toy. As the meeting dragged on Pirate Pete kept tapping it quietly against his hand as the principal spoke. Finally, clearly agitated, the principal spun to face him and asked, "Why do you have a sword?" Deadpan the teacher replied, "Behaviour management, sir."

Sometimes instinct takes over and we lash out in irrational ways despite all of our training to react otherwise. I admit that I once bashed a little girl on top of the head. Now this is not what it sounds like. It was not intentional or vicious. This little jumping jack was sitting on the floor at my elbow and kept popping up to share her every thought. She did this by springing to her feet, turning in the air as she did so to face the class and spewing forth her inaccurate musings. I had asked her several times to take her turn, put her hand up to share and for god's sake stop jumping up every few seconds to yell out her every thought. Even the other kids were becoming annoyed.

So, when I caught her out of the corner of my eye beginning to rise up for the umpteenth time I brought my hand down towards the top of her head to keep her seated. The intent on my part was a gentle hand on top of her head to keep her in place, but the swiftness of this action paired with the sheer force generated by the speed of her skyward launch resulted in an audible smack to the top of the head. The kids gasped. I apologised profusely and bouncy girl stayed put. I went straight to the principal as soon as there was a break and confessed to the bashing. The principal reassured me that with no malicious intent, no injury and no complaint from the child I would be fine.

As parents of students who occasionally (or frequently, depending on which child we're talking about) required disciplinary action at school my

206

husband and I rarely questioned the offending action, but sometimes disagreed with the punishment. One fine day in middle school our youngest son decided to jump off the second floor balcony and had the misfortune of landing – soft-footed and panther-like though it was – right next to the French teacher. Now, the French teacher at this school was renowned for announcing to her classes on the first day of school each year that she was the meanest teacher in the school. True to her word, she saw no redeeming value in the athletic ability displayed by our son's fine stunt. Unable to claim he "didn't do it" after such a spectacular entrance to the ground floor foyer, he was hauled into the principal's office and suspended from school for a week.

When my husband and I questioned the suspension the administration circled the wagons and said, "We are sorry to have to tell you this, but we have several witnesses to this act and he DID jump from the second floor."

Surprised at their misreading of our displeasure we replied, "Oh no, we don't disagree with that. We completely believe that he jumped. Frankly we are surprised it wasn't a back flip. What we do disagree with is the suspension." We knew our son and giving him a week off of school was quite possibly in his opinion the best thing that had ever happened to him. We could read his mind and we were quite sure he was thinking, "Hmmm. A week for the balcony! What could I get for the roof?"

Our youngest was one of those kids that I spoke of earlier that needs the rules very clearly defined. There is an infinite number of ways to break the rules without even knowing it if you are a risk taker. Who says you can't shove a stick in the bubbler (drinking fountain for USA) to alter the direction of the water? Why can't you jump from the second floor balcony to the lower foyer if that is within your skill set? On 'camo day' is it not in fact 'camo' if you strap branches to your clothes, climb a tree and gently drop twigs onto fellow students below? Our son, who did all of these and more, is now a qualified stunt man by trade. Had we completely squashed his natural passion for movement, this may not have come to pass.

Rules are tricky business these days. Elementary schools back in my day had four basic rules: Don't hurt people. Don't talk out of turn. Don't lie. Don't damage property. Consequences for breaching those rules included: A glare, a smack, some unpleasant time with the principal, parental involvement, or possible suspension or expulsion.

Since rules are considered negative now we have *essential agreements*. These essential agreements are decided on as a group and signed by all students and the teacher. They can only be worded in positive terms such as 'keep your hands and feet to yourself'. Consequently they can end up somewhat vague. Be respectful. Be safe. Be kind. Let's just add world peace and call it good.

As with my own beloved two youngest, often students find creative ways to get around the rules. There are an infinite number of actions that a child can take that are not specifically against the rules. Where is the rule written that says, 'Thou shall not wet a paper towel, roll it tight and try to sharpen it in the electric pencil sharpener'?

I once had to create a new rule in my first grade classroom to address a fascinating new inquiry activity involving the guts of markers being put into water bottles to make many hued waters. Now in this new age we are not to say, "For Christ's sake stop destroying your markers and manufacturing toxic concoctions that stain the blankety-blank carpet when you spill it." In new-speak the rule becomes, 'Please keep the colour producing spongy bit inside your marker at all times'.

Our youngest son was particularly adept at testing the waters when it came to school rules. The principal of the primary school in Australia that all four of our kids attended was a fair, but stern disciplinarian. He usually stopped a questionable action, made it abundantly clear why that was not within the scope of acceptable activities, issued a stern warning complete with possible consequences, then waited for the kid to do it again.

One day when our clown was five years old he was deftly directing sprays of water from the outdoor bubbler onto passing classmates. Mr. C calmly explained to our little guy that his thumb did not belong in that stream of water and fun as it might be on that hot day he needed to desist from that activity. "*Keep your thumb out of the bubbler*." Got it.

Not more than three minutes later Mr. C saw that shimmering arc of water make a direct hit to the eye of an unsuspecting passer-by. However, at the helm was another child who looked as shocked as the soaked one. As it turns out our little innovative one had stuck a small twig in the waterspout so that he did not in fact have his thumb in the bubbler. Hence this action was not technically against the rule he had just had clearly explained to him. Keep your thumb out of the bubbler left room for interpretation. Of course this lack of extrapolation didn't fly with Mr. C and the resulting intervention was the reason for us knowing this story.

Violence is the one area that always needs firm and swift action. I have found that calm intervention works best unless the child is swinging from the monkey bars. While on playground duty once I was summoned by other children to intervene in the antics of a known violent perpetrator who was swinging from the monkey bars and lashing out at all comers with his feet. Foolishly, I walked calmly over to this little monster crooning, "Here, let me help you get down." He responded by pulling his knees up to his chest and launching with both feet full into my chest knocking me to the ground. Having shocked himself as much as the kids around him, he jumped down and headed straight for his classroom. I spent the next couple of weeks in back rehab, while the kicker did a stint of in-school suspension.

At the end of the day all we can really do is follow the school policy on discipline to the best of our ability and try to believe that in most cases kids do want to please. Take each incident as it comes, trust your gut and don't expect that any of the strategies developed by experts who have never dealt with more than one child at a time are going to work with this particular child at this particular time.

My advice:

1. Never hit a child intentionally.
2. Try to believe in good intent.
3. Never approach kickers from the front.

Subbing or Relief Teaching

Substitute teaching is another whole art in itself. I subbed (relief taught) for several years when my kids were young and will end my teaching career the same way. Despite being more of the mellow type I handled the challenge well and enjoyed it immensely. Because I managed to inherit my Grandma Bessie's easy-going nature I found that unusual situations, cheeky kids, or total lack of direction from the classroom teacher couldn't easily throw me. You will encounter one or all of those things each and every day. It is a rough job, but it has some serious upsides.

The best thing about relief teaching is the lack of homework for the teacher. People who are not teachers or married to teachers really have no idea how much time is spent outside of the classroom planning lessons, grading papers and tests, recording scores and crunching data. The beauty of relief teaching is that you don't have to do any of that. To me it seems a little like being a grandparent. You get to have the fun of spending time with kids and then they go home.

The other big perk of substitute teaching is the lack of any long-term repercussions for you. If you let some things slide it doesn't cause any chinks in your armour.

Let's say a kid fails to turn in his paper. Not my problem. A kid chews all the erasers off the ends of his pencils. I don't care. Now, don't get me wrong, I will try to keep everything going as it should, but if kids have chronic behaviours that are not causing disruption or safety concerns, I do not have to find a solution or work out an intervention plan for that kid.

The final, and most appealing for those who look after their own well-being first and foremost, is the 'no thank you' clause. When called for a class that has previously left you with a bald spot where you ripped out your own hair you have the right to decline the offer. You will want to tread lightly with most of the harried and frantic teachers or administrators stuck with the horrendous responsibility of finding last minute replacements for an ill teacher. They can and do sometimes take the rejection personally. However, since this is a perk of the job, I wholly endorse turning down jobs that will shorten your lifespan.

There was a social studies class at one American high school that I refused to ever sub in again. I was a veteran teacher with more than twenty years of experience during one of our international transition periods when I took two days on this particular class. The seventeen and eighteen-year-old students in this class had to have been part of some sort of social experiment. I am convinced they were brought in from a juvenile detention facility and the whole rude and horrendous affair was being filmed with hidden cameras. However, when I checked in with the office at the end of the second day and told them I would not be back on that class ever again they were quite dismayed. The office ladies begged me to stay because the regular teacher had just had her *stress leave* extended to the end of the term. I employed the 'no thank you' clause and sprinted out the door.

From the other side of the story as a classroom teacher, no matter how well you train your class there is a good chance they will still test the boundaries with the sub when you are away. Here is an actual excerpt from a note I received from a very seasoned sub that had my first grade class one fine spring day. "*OMG! Rough day: Susie and Alice cut up a bunch of things, dropped them on the floor and escaped to the bathroom without asking. Jane filled her mouth with water and pretended to throw up on John's desk! This was all before nine AM!!*" She went on to explain why most of the items in my sub plans were not accomplished. Actually, this was a pretty good class and a very competent sub. It is just that sometimes kids feel obliged to test the boundaries when they get the chance and the regular teacher's absence is the natural time to do that.

The sub's best defence is the threat of teacher reprisal. The threat goes like this: *So help me god, if you don't cease and desist I shall have to pummel you*. No – wait. That's not it. The threat is: *I **will** be leaving a note for your teacher*. Now the majority of kids know this is true and they know that hell hath no fury like the wrath

214

of a teacher who gets a bad note from the sub. They know that the next day will be one to be faking a fever at home.

I personally really enjoyed relief teaching back in the 90s in Australia. Back then if a teacher was ill they took the day off. They were not expected to rush in early and write out plans for the day. Nor did they have twenty-four hour a day access to their job via e-mail, Google docs, or interconnectedness so they could control the school day through a fever induced fog. This left me to create a stimulating day of learning through my own wits and imagination. I loved it!

During those relief-teaching years I had an actual physical bag of tricks. This was a shoulder bag full of themed one-day units, which mostly addressed environmental issues and the plight of indigenous peoples around the world. I kept a notebook in which I recorded which lessons I had covered in various classes so that when I returned to the same class on future visits I did not repeat myself. Because these units were unique and unrelated to the daily slog most kids were engaged and trouble was very minimal.

A sense of humour is critical. Recently I had the pleasure of spending an evening at a pub trivia night with some of my son's friends who had been in classes that I had relief taught in twenty some years ago. One of them was reminiscing about a time when I was on his year six class and I let the kids swing from the rafters. The real story was that some of the taller and more athletic kids in the class could jump up and grab the low open ceiling rafters. This seemed a rather unsafe activity with legs flailing about amongst other students' heads.

Sensing this could be a potentially enticing incentive, I made the kids an offer. Rather than spend the day reminding them to keep their feet on the ground, I promised them that if everybody finished their work and behaved in a polite and sensible manner for the remainder of the day, I would allow rafter swinging for the last ten minutes. At 2:50 p.m. we pushed all the tables and chairs aside and the little monkeys swung from the rafters to their hearts' content for ten minutes. Apparently this is a major treasured memory for this thirty-something grown up firefighter. I'm glad.

These days the expectation is that the relief teacher follows the program if at all possible, so that the kids don't miss out on the planned curriculum. When I retire from full time teaching I will be old enough to boldly do it my own way again and if they want a fearless relief teacher who is unflappable they will not worry if their own lessons are used or not. The kids will learn and we will have some laughs. I am looking forward to it.

Relief teaching advice:

1. Do not attempt this if you are anxious of the unknown.

2. Do not take a rough class more than twice if you pulled even a little hair out of your head during or after the experience.

3. Have fun with the kids within reasonable bounds.

What Doesn't Kill You Makes You Stronger

In a weak moment of financial need while living in Colorado I accepted a job as an eighth grade science teacher. In most schools in the USA this means teaching chemistry and physics. The sheer thought of this combination of chemicals, fire and adolescent hormones would be absolutely terrifying to a rational person. Without going into detail about our family financial situation at the time, I was no longer a rational person at that particular point in August just before the school year was about to start. So rather than spend another year substitute teaching, I accepted the offer and began a year of personal enlightenment.

Bear in mind that the following recollections are written with the utmost respect and admiration for those teachers who have chosen to tame the tempest that is the pubescent pupil. These people, misguided and idealistic as they may be, serve a higher calling than any policeman, firefighter or active duty military person. Yet, they seem to be somewhat normal people to the untrained eye. They walk amongst us every day.

With minimal practice you can begin to recognize middle school teachers outside of their usual habitat.

The novices have a distinctive edginess to them. They look ordinary except for the occasional nervous twitch or barely perceptible darting of the eyes. This rapid eye movement is brought on by the same survival instincts that keep these troopers from sitting still for more than a few seconds. The well-seasoned veterans still have a measure of protective armour, but their eyes are more glazed over and they are strong – really strong. Don't mess with these vets.

Teaching middle school science was literally trial by fire. Because I have a previous horticulture degree (and the required number of science credits to have earned said degree) the State of Colorado deemed me highly qualified to teach science. Never mind that it had been more than thirty years since I had balanced a chemical equation or lit a Bunsen burner. I was hired one week and teaching chemistry lab the next. It turns out that lab safety, how to light a Bunsen burner and the procedure for melting and bending little rods of glass never really leaves you. However, after teaching primary grades for more than twenty years, my methods needed a quick adjustment. No adoring gazes here. I was being judged.

The first thing I realised at this affluent school was that the teenagers in these science classes singlehandedly supported the global economy. The number of cell phones, iPods (yes, I said iPod), skateboards, designer clothes, and other name brand accessories was staggering. Because they owned the material goods of the world they felt they reserved the right to run the world.

One of my aunts used to say that children temporarily leave the human race at around thirteen and hopefully re-enter again at around seventeen or eighteen years of age. Actually what she used to say was that they should be put in a cage at this point and not released until at least four years had passed – but that was just her particular bias. Seriously though, the whole cage thing would have worked so much better than the twirling stools in that chemistry lab.

Here is the equation I was working with: hormones + fire + chemicals + spinning stools = holy shit! Now add attitude. So, now we have the spinning bundles of hormones handling fire and chemicals with an attitude. Attitude is an interesting word. The meaning when referring to teenagers is undeniably negative. 'She has an attitude' means she is in a perpetually foul mood and looks at all adults and most of her peers with disdain.

I recall with fondness the daily antics of one young undersized would-be thug who had taken on the personal mission of finding some way to embarrass me. He was in his element the week we began sex education. His questions were direct and graphic. If appropriate I answered them directly. But if not, I told him he would need to ask his parents.

After a week of continuously asking uncomfortable questions, I told him he was not going to embarrass me no matter how hard he tried. I explained that I had been teaching for nearly twenty-five years, given birth to four kids, raised four teenagers and worked in dozens of schools with every age level in several different states and countries. Above all, I had survived high school and college in the 70s and there was very little possibility that he could fluster me with questions about sexual acts. Thus deflated, he returned to spinning his chair and tossing his hair out of his eyes.

Middle school girls are perpetually on their period. These circumstances conveniently allow them to leave the room urgently or arrive late with the 'girl business' excuse. Unless we were to keep a detailed flow chart (pun intended) we teachers can't possibly track it well enough to question the frequency with which these periods occur.

Boys don't quite understand the complexity of all of this, but don't question the privilege afforded their female counterparts. Far better to let this gross unfairness slide than to delve into the mysterious realm of the female needs. Moodiness is just part of the package. Of course, this is part of the fascination for boys. It is like trying to navigate through a minefield. Some days it is worth it for the adrenaline rush of attempting communication with the menstruating ones and on other days it is far better to just take the path of least resistance and let it all slide.

The actual labs themselves were an adventure. The first hurdle after the spinning stools was convincing thirteen and fourteen-year-olds girls to wear those huge, ugly, plastic safety goggles. I put them on. I smiled. It didn't matter that I was willing to look dorky. I was old and no longer required to even pretend to be cool. The girls however, had no intention of going to their next class with red suction marks ringing their eyes like raccoons.

The next challenge was to convince my new juvenile friends that they needed to follow my directions to the letter if they did not wish to catch on fire, throw up in front of their peers, or worse (to steal a line from Hermione) – be kicked out of class. The final and biggest obstacle to science lab success was to find a way to make it relevant to their lives.

In a misguided attempt to accomplish this goal and live up to the International Baccalaureate ideals of true inquiry based learning, I decided to have a discovery day. This was an opportunity for inquiring minds to design and conduct their own chemical experiment. This idea was met with an admirable level of enthusiasm and the students came up with some interesting inquiries.

I scrutinized each proposed experiment for safety and let them loose. The joy of the unknown pervaded the room. Most results involved a substance consistency change, colour change, or total flop. Inevitably one experiment involved a spectacular explosion.

Lucky for my hapless junior scientists and my career this gooey multicoloured substance blew straight up and adhered itself to the ceiling. After an unprecedented five seconds of silence I broke first with an inappropriate giggle. Then clambering back to my teacher status I lamely declared, "And that, my friends, is why we wear our safety goggles."

As mentioned in a previous chapter, my first ever full time teaching position came out of the blue one day when I was called to take over a Year Two class just three days into the school year. The teacher had unexpectedly just up and quit. That should have been a clue for me to run away... fast. I didn't. As described earlier I was able to get that group of ragamuffins on track, but the class was graced with the presence of a little charmer I shall call Dick. Now little Dick was combative and irritable all day – every day. It actually baffled me that a child of only seven years old could be so completely out of control.

This mystery was solved one day when I was having the opening chat with my kids and I heard Dick screaming obscenities at the top of his lungs outside. As I looked out the window I could see him swinging a big stick at somebody he had trapped in the recessed school entryway. Fearing that he was actually about to kill somebody right there at the front door, I dashed to the rescue of the victim under attack only to find that the person cowering in the corner was Dick's mother! She was pleading, "Please, honey. Put the stick down." He was countering with, "I hate your guts, you *&#." Obviously, we had some parental control issues coming into play here.

In the interest of preservation of life and limb for the other thirty-one kids in the class the principal hired a minder for this little cherub. I called this man my bouncer. I have never been sure of the validity of this alleged program or where exactly this angel in the form of a 6'6" three hundred and fifty pound gorilla actually came from. The story given to me by the principal was that this man was participating in an ex-con program of rehabilitation. Whatever. He was a saviour.

When the bouncer said, "Sit!" Dick sat. When the bouncer said, "Shut up!" Dick shut up. Unfortunately, this was not enough to curb criminal activity outside of school and Dick was eventually sent to a reform school. As soon as I realised the implications of Dick's departure I scurried to the principal, dropped to my knees and begged for the retention of my beloved bouncer. As it turned out he was contracted for one full school term and he remained on duty in my class happily scrunching his enormous body into those little tiny chairs and team-taught with me for the rest of that term.

How hard can it be to manage six-year-olds? Bloody hard my friend if there is no parental follow through. One year I had a first grade class that challenged my inherently non-violent nature. For the first time in my career a class was actually stressing me out.

One day I took the morning off to go to the dentist. It was just a routine cleaning, but as it neared completion I found myself recalling a common adage when people really have a strong eversion to something. The saying goes, 'I would rather have a root canal'. I honestly sat there in that dental chair considering requesting a root canal rather than return for the afternoon with that class. Realistically I knew they would deem me in need of some psychiatric help if I pleaded, "Could you please do a root canal now? Just pick a tooth – any tooth."

My advice:

1. Don't let anybody convince you that middle school kids are real people.
2. Accept a bouncer if one is offered and don't question where he came from.
3. Have a go at the tough stuff, but for God's sake don't stay there.

Body Fluids and Injuries

If you faint at the sight of blood, gag when you smell vomit or see boogers, or are averse to body fluids, do not teach the primary grades. I don't know what else to tell you, but you *will* encounter body fluids. Assuming you are an adult the chances are that you are familiar with the various types of body fluids, but as way of a quick review – they come in clear, yellow, green, red and multihued colours. They can be chunky, slimy, slippery, or stinky and come in various viscosities. They can leak out or be much more forceful in their expulsion.

This is a short direct chapter aimed at helping you recognize the signs and impart some advice as to evasive action that you can employ.

First rule of operation – always believe a child who tells you he is about to spew, pee, poop, chuck, or otherwise introduce human liquids into the environment. Even if this is a ploy to get out of some school task, it is better to err on the side of caution when it comes to fluids.

Shy children are the ones to watch. They often only give you the slightest hint or quietly prep you for the impending event in such an apologetic or offhand way

226

that it does not properly prepare you for the upcoming calamity. They also will not admonish you afterwards with, "I told you so." But, their eyes will.

A few years ago at the end of the day one of my quietest first graders tapped me gently on the hip and said, "My tummy feels funny." My lame reply as I continued to dismiss kids to get their belongings to go home was, "It's OK, honey. Just let your mom know when you get home." His response was to projectile vomit with a vigour rivalling the little girl in *The Exorcist*. He achieved a direct hit in the centre of his desktop causing a splash pattern that included most of the desks within a half-mile radius.

This epic expulsion was outdone recently by a kindergartener in our cohort. Our three classes were lined up to come in from recess when queasy little guy told his teacher he thought he might throw up. Being an experienced teacher, she quickly grabbed his shoulders and turned him away from his classmates. He immediately tilted his head back and began to imitate an agricultural grade irrigation gun spraying his stomach contents in a huge arc. Despite her own rapidly advancing gag reflex my colleague continued to slowly rotate queasy guy's body position as he flung his head around to avoid the spew hitting anybody or anything but the pavement.

When the carnage ended we sent the poor kid to sick bay and ushered the rest of the kids inside. It was once we were inside and away from the putrid puddle outside that we realised we did not get away unscathed. The kids were all clear but us teachers had to wash our feet and shoes in the sink. They never mention this in university teacher prep courses.

A few years ago after three years in first grade and more than thirty years of classroom teaching I had finally acquired a cute rug with the ABCs and adorable pictures on it. I excitedly spread it on the floor in front of my chair for the kids to sit on. I was quite stuck on it. It looked pretty cute. I kid you not, that very same day a child peed on it. Nobody in this class had peed their pants all year and certainly not this particular child. But I guess it was a bit like a puppy on a new rug. It just had to be done.

While on the subject of pee, my second or third week of teaching PE I was outside with kindergarteners playing a running game when a clearly agitated and red-faced boy stamped up to me and pointed at his shoe. Through his tears he yelled, "Bobby peed on my shoe!" Seeing as this was wrong on several levels, I corralled Bobby and asked him if this transgression was true. He admitted that it was. "Why?" I asked, genuinely baffled. "Because, I had to pee," was his matter-of-fact reply.

I explained to him that there were several reasons that this just didn't really fit in with school policy. 1) We pee only in the toilets while at school. 2) It is distressing to have your shoe peed on. 3) His classmate's shoe was now disgusting. He responded by reaching down and attempted to wipe the pee off his classmate's shoe as he sincerely apologised. Then the two boys grabbed hands (yes, the pee wiping hand) and skipped off happily together.

Sneezing is a big body fluid spreader. First graders generally aim for your face. Not intentionally of course. It is just that when you lean down to hear their complaint about not feeling well you generally put your face in the direct path. Teachers can tell you the exact moment that they contracted an illness. If not a face misting, the alternative is often a big stringy booger that either hangs there a while and moves up and down with the child's breathing or gets wiped away by the child's hand.

The favoured wiping technique by the younger ones is to smear it off to the side where it can dry on the cheek. Less popular, but still in regular use is to start at the end of the booger and wipe upwards with the heal of the hand. This wipe can extend on up past the nose, between the eyes and into the hairline. The obvious solution to all of this is to have lots of tissue boxes around during allergy and cold seasons. Less obvious is the need to have deliberate, direct and extensive training in how to use and dispose of tissues.

Blood. There are so many reasons to bleed in primary school. Skinned knees and bloody noses are the front-runners, closely followed by paper cuts and picked scabs. Reaction to blood is highly variable and unpredictable. One child can come up to you with the tiniest almost imperceptible paper cut and be wailing at the top of his lungs while another is quietly leaning over the sink haemorrhaging from the nose with alarming volume, pressing paper towels to her face while assuring concerned classmates that she is just fine.

No matter how parents react at home you as the teacher can somewhat influence the reaction at school by your response to the injury or unexpected illness. As I previously mentioned, my mother's standard response as we stood before her with a missing lower limb or growing an enormous unicorn horn was to glance absentmindedly at the deformed body part and soothe us with, "It's OK, honey. It will feel better when it stops hurting."

We usually thanked her, returned her warm hug and limped back outside to resume play. Later that evening, she might look at the purple egg on our forehead or the gaping hole in our flesh and say, "Hummm, maybe we should have got stitches in that."

A little history here explains this lax attitude toward bodily injury. When my mother was five years old in 1937, she was playing with some of her siblings and little friends in her front yard in Minneapolis. As it happens, the teenage boy next door was simultaneously trying out his new rifle.

As luck would have it, he shot my mother in the head. As the family story goes: the bullet 'merely grazed' her forehead. As Mom's enraged father chased the shooter down the street my grandmother carried her bleeding but conscious daughter inside, laid her on the couch, daubed the blood up with a towel and calmly declared that all was well, because, "Look. You can see where the bullet went in right here and then came out again just over here. She will be fine."

My mother's low-key approach trained me to not overreact to all the little injuries that happen daily. If a child complains that their knee hurts I usually offer amputation as a solution. This is so outrageous that they usually laugh and concede that they will be fine. The same goes for fingers and toes. If they say that their shoulder hurts when they spin their arm around above their head, I suggest that perhaps they don't do that.

Aside from wearing a HAZMAT suit or simply a mask and rubber gloves, there is really not a whole lot you can do to avoid body fluids in the primary school environment.

Advice on body fluids:
1. Always – and I mean always – have tissues and Band-Aids in your pockets.
2. Never show your own shock or horror at an injury.
3. Go right ahead and express disgust at the boogers. They need to learn.

Perspectives

Anybody who has spent much time around young children realises that their perception of their world, and the people in their world, comes from a whole different realm of reality than those of us humans with considerably more years residing on this planet. They have a vastly unique perspective on life.

The little ones see things in a very pure and concrete way. Whatever they don't understand is magical, fascinating and worthy of their undivided attention. What they think they do understand is very straightforward and they have no hesitation about sharing their view or random observation with you and the class.

Your challenge is to change your own perspective frequently. Squat right down on their level. Tilt your head. Blink your eyes and look again. Mostly, just try to think outside the box that most of us tend to shimmy further into as we age.

My daughter once read a Facebook post from a fellow teacher friend. This first grade teacher was thanking her principal for coming into her classroom and explaining to the boys in her class that the freaky *Chucky Doll* character did not in fact haunt the stalls in the boys' bathroom, so nobody needed to poop in the urinals. This is an example of logical thinking by young children. If Chucky is indeed in the stalls, then it is best to stay out of them and the urinal is a much better place to poop than the floor.

These kinds of irrational fears can take hold in a class or a school without our knowledge. You might obverse some mildly bizarre behaviour, only to uncover that some odd counterculture has developed unbeknownst to you.

At one school my fourth grade classroom was on the second floor. The staircase was one of those open ones where you can see through the steps. Between the last landing and the ground floor there was an open space used to store spare desks, etc.

I noticed a couple of months into the school year that kids took the last half dozen or more steps at a very fast clip on the way down or they launched themselves off the landing at great risk of life and limb. On the way up they approached with trepidation, peered cautiously between the steps and then sprinted up to the landing. This was most definitely not safe behaviour. Athletic as it might be, it needed to stop.

So one day, modelling my best inquiry based learning, I asked the kids why they feared the lower steps. They were very matter-of-fact with the answer. "Well, Mrs. Davis, *they* say that sometimes the shadow guys take stuff and sometimes they grab your ankles through the steps if you go too slow or especially if you stop." Shadow guys? What?

"Since when?" I queried. With slow sincere shaking of their tussled little heads they replied, "Well, we are not real sure. We think the shadow guys started hanging out ever since Zoe lost her shoe down there." OK now we were getting somewhere. I did remember the day Zoe lost her shoe down off the landing and despite everyone's best efforts we never did find it. So honestly, who am I to question the existence of shadow guys?

Sometimes the actual content of your lessons is completely lost due to the focus of attention being shifted elsewhere. Back in my relief teaching days in Australia I was delivering a lesson on electricity to a class of year two students. Predictably, the lesson was way over the heads of seven and eight-year olds and they were fading fast. There were two reasons that I didn't bail on the whole pointless endeavour. First, it was the only item on the teacher's note that she had specifically asked me to please try and cover for sure. Second, and more importantly, I had spotted one child with her eyes fixed on my face. Every fibre of her tiny body was a picture of pure concentration as she strove to understand what she was seeing and hearing.

As her classmates squirmed and fidgeted, this one beautiful child alone stared directly at my face. When I finished reading and explaining the little science booklet and asked if anybody had any questions, her little hand instantly shot into the air. "Awesome," I thought, "I have engaged at least one child in this lesson."

When I called on my eager little enquirer she smiled sweetly at me and asked, "Why are your teeth crooked?" I don't even remember what I replied.

In addition to having crooked teeth, which I have always had, in recent years my increasingly wrinkled hands, neck and face have come under scrutiny by students. The invention of the document camera to replace overhead projectors has made teaching easier, but the drawback is that whatever one puts under a document camera is magnified in all its glory and projected on the screen for all to see. The first time I used a document camera, my fourth grade class gasped in a perfectly synchronised intake of breath.

Still reasonably impressed with this technology myself, I swung my head around towards the whiteboard to look at the diagram I had drawn the night before and was now obviously causing such a wonder-filled response from my young charges. At the same moment that I caught sight of my half century old, large veined, age spotted hands at roughly six times their actual size, I also heard one of the students whisper, "Whoa, look at those hands."

My favourite story concerning my advancing age involved two kindergarteners in my PE class in Colorado a few years ago. I was teaching the kids how to hurdle over little miniature hurdles and one of the little boys was phenomenal. In coaching Track and Field for over twenty years, I had rarely seen anyone, much less a five-year-old, pick it up so fast.

I praised this little mini athlete and he responded by unequivocally stating that he was going to be an Olympic hurdler one day. Impressed by his confidence, I assured him, "I believe you will be and I will be watching you in the Olympics in about eighteen years!"

His classmate, who had been standing beside me staring up at my face, shook his head with a 'who's she kidding' look of disbelief and emphatically declared, "Nah. You'll be dead in eighteen years." Call it like you see it my friend.

I began to notice this whole focus on my apparent agedness a few years ago when a colleague Laura and I were asked by a third grader if I was Laura's mother. Seeing as Laura is only about ten years younger than me, I was amused, but also mildly annoyed. I would have been willing to laugh it off if Laura hadn't patted the darling child on the head and said, "Yes!" To which I yelled, "No!"

Yes. No. Yes. No. We volleyed back and forth and left the child confused. To this day, Laura greets me as "Mommy!" and calls my daughters "Sis" and my sons "Bro." She's not quite sure what to call my husband.

Before my apparently obvious and ever so public slide into the geriatric group, student perceptions of me were more aimed at what I did, or ate, or wore. As I mentioned earlier, I am a pretty casual dresser. As a classroom teacher I usually wore jeans and nice shirts or a sweater. As a PE teacher, of course I wore sweatpants and t-shirts or sweatshirts. So when I wore anything else, like a skirt or even nice pants, all the little girls would gush about how beautiful I looked.

The day of my oldest son's high school graduation breakfast I took the morning off. I was teaching PE at that time and when I arrived back in the gym in a nice dress and shoes without traction soles, the choir was practicing on the stage. They stopped dead, slack jawed and stunned. The music teacher turned around and spotted me in all my feminine glory. After she picked herself up off the floor, she asked me to please stay in the PE office until I was dressed appropriately because I was distracting the students. To the students and evidently the other teachers, I was a PE teacher and wearing the same clothes that other teachers wore daily was just not acceptable.

An encounter typical of the direct nature of conversation you come to expect from six-year-olds involved a child who was writing a story about me. She looked up at the top of my head and asked sweetly, "Would you call the colour of your hair more grey or white?" It is sandy blonde, sweetie! Sandy blonde!

Recently one of my kindergarteners was working on cutting out a creation next to me when he turned and asked me, "How old are you again, Mrs. Davis?" When I replied that I was sixty-three years old he said, "So you were alive when the dinosaurs were still around, right?" He is lucky HE is still alive.

During reading groups one day the sweetest little guy in my kinder class gazed up at me and softly queried, "Mrs. Davis?"

I replied in an equally gentle voice, "Yes, sweetheart, what is it?"

He stared intently at my face and declared, "You are really lucky ya know – to still have all your teeth at your age."

To which I rolled my lips over my teeth to feign toothlessness and replied, "Thanks, darling, sorry you don't have yours."

Little kids are the best. I admire the honesty. The beauty of all this honesty is I never have to wonder if I look tired, have food on my face, or stuff in my teeth, because the kids will tell me. One particularly hot day just a couple of weeks into teaching kindergarten, I wore a cool summer dress that came to just above my knees. Seeing my wrinkly, loose skinned knees for the first time, one of my darlings smiled, drew in his breath in admiration and told me how closely they resembled the knees of an elephant. Thanks kid.

My advice:
1. Embrace the odd perspectives.
2. Never ask for clarification.
3. Grow thicker skin.

I know! I know!

Most young children are eager to answer and not afraid to be wrong. If the right risk free environment is in place, they will astound you with their thoughts.

Word definitions are the best. Ask a kid to define an unknown word and you will get the most amazing answers. Did you know that a *column* is that weird little guy in Lord of the Rings that is always saying, "my precious"? Did you know that a *Coat of Arms* is a type of skin tone? One of my kindergarteners confidently answered when I asked the class if they knew what a summary was. "I know! I know! A summary is a special boat that can go under water." When asked on a math test to tell how to know when you need to regroup one student responded, "When I need to regroup is when I get stressed out."

I coordinated our school garden in Colorado and one day one of my little six-year olds burst into the room in the morning with a treasure grasped tightly in his tiny fist. "Mrs. Davis, Mrs. Davis, I have a seed for the garden!" He opened his hand to reveal a smooth whitish seed about the size of a cupcake sprinkle. Bending down for a closer look and to give the seed the attention it deserved I asked my little gardener what kind of seed it was. With his giant eyes growing even wider, he declared, "It's a bagel seed!"

Most of these small pearls of wisdom emerge in response to a situation, a prompt, a question, or deep thought over time about a particular subject, but sometimes they just pop into a child's head. Just before Thanksgiving one year when the kids were making those little hand tracing turkeys one of my little boys rushed up to me nearly knocking me over in his haste. His glasses were skidded off his nose and one shoe was off. He had that look about him of a person who had just had a serious revelation. If that were indeed the case here, it would be not only be a revelation, but the first coherent thought this particular child had ever expressed to me. As he picked glue off his fingers and looked at me over the top rim of his glasses he declared, "One day when you get to heaven, don't be surprised to see a LOT of turkeys."

Random thoughts can emerge at any moment. You try to make the connection to the topic at hand, but sometimes you just can't. At least turkey boy was working on Thanksgiving crafts when he had his heaven revelation. The child I am about to quote appeared to be totally oblivious to her surroundings the vast majority of the time, so when she raised her hand during a discussion about pulleys and levers I was stoked. I smiled at her and asked her what she thought was about to happen when we pulled on the rope. She grinned back and declared, "My grandma has a parrot named Cheeky that calls you asshole when you touch her cage." Now isn't that interesting darling.

Since they think they know more than they do, every now and again you come across an expert. When I announced one day that we were going to begin a soccer unit one eager little boy raised his hand and simultaneously began uttering the "Oh! Oh! Oh!" that signals extreme desire to share what is most forefront in the brain. I called on him and quivering with excitement he declared, "I know this game! I have been playing soccer for eight years!"

Wow. I looked at him and queried, "You have? How old are you?"

He beamed at me and replied, "Five-years-old." Neat trick.

There was a series of TV commercials selling high speed internet airing in the USA a few years ago where an adult interviewer sat in a tiny little child-sized chair at a table with young children and asked them questions about which is better; faster or slower. The kids came up with a plethora of bizarre answers. One answer involved a lengthy scenario involving werewolves and the need for speed to not become one.

The interviewer stared at this imaginative little girl and replied, "Wh... what?" My daughter (who was teaching second grade at the time) and I were giggling as we watched these hilarious interviews one night and then reminded my husband that these amusing scenarios were in fact our daily reality. Everyday in reading group, or on the floor during whole group time, or returning from the wide world that is recess, we heard these pearls of wisdom. Pure joy.

One day I was math tutoring a little kindergarten boy in Colorado and he announced that he was moving to another country. When I asked him which country he said, "I can't remember, but if you will just tell me all the places in the world – but not this one – I will tell you when you get it right." Awesome. How hard could that be? In an attempt to narrow the field somewhat (and living as we did in a military town) I asked him if his dad was military. He said he was, so I began guessing countries with USA bases. Tiring of my ignorance, he finally giggled, "No silly. Texas!" Oh, that other country!

My move to first grade after several years on the upper grades was a mind-altering adventure into a world that was a delightful mixture of literal interpretation and fantasy belief. Santa Claus, the Easter Bunny, and the Tooth Fairy coexisted nicely with the solar system. One could grow bagels from seeds and cows could jump over the moon.

One day, one of my students came to school all excited because it was Mommy's birthday. When I asked her how old her mom was going to be she declared, "She's ninety- five!"

Wow, impressive. "Really?" I replied. "How old is your Dad?"

"Oh, he is twenty-nine," she sweetly replied. Now I wonder who supplied those numbers.

Returning to my classroom with my class one afternoon, we encountered a little boy from my previous year's class. He was standing in the room looking decidedly perplexed. When I asked him if he needed something he shifted his gaze to me and slowly shook his head no. "Well, can I help you with anything then?" I probed. Again he slowly and vaguely signalled no. Finally realising what may have happened I asked, "Did you come back to my room by mistake?"

His eyes lit up and he jubilantly shouted, "That's it!" Then he hurriedly scurried out of my room and on down the hall to second grade. To borrow a line from Seinfeld – 'Senility is going to be a smooth transition for that kid'.

The trick when confronted with children's wisdom is to nod sagely, try not to judge and say, "Well, thank you for that. I will take it under consideration." Here are three pearls of wisdom from my first graders. You might want to take some of them under consideration.

1. Rapunzel should always line up at the end of the line. *Very wise .*
2. Poop takes longer, so I might not be back as quick as normal. *Can be true.*
3. We should just get a goat to keep the floor clean. *It would be well nourished.*

I Done Me Grammar Good

Despite all of our best efforts, not every child will soak in all of the teachings we provide. There are a multitude of reasons for this, but if we see the humour in the mistakes and teach the kids to do the same we can all learn and maybe get some entertainment at the same time.

One day at a school in Australia our principal came across a student running out of school a minute or so early. One of the traditions back-in-the-day at some of the schools I used to teach at in Australia was that if a child had done something good, kind, or particularly clever he could earn an 'early mark'. This meant he could leave school a minute or so early – a big deal to a primary age student. Well, when the principal stopped this particular child and asked him why he was out early, he replied, "I done me grammar good, sir." What a proud moment at our school.

One of my all time favourite math answers was produced in my first grade class. The story problem read: *There were eight polar bears on an ice floe. Two dove into the water. How many were left?* There was even a picture of eight polar bears on the ice, so the kids could just cross off the two that dove in the water. The answer written neatly in the space provided and in the format I had taught (and spelled correctly) was: "*100 + 10 = 158 There were 158 polar bears left.*" What the . . ?

A failure like this notwithstanding, one has to admire the enthusiasm of our youngest pupils. Even when they are dead wrong they often will argue their point to the bitter end. *There are so 158 bears, because there couldn't possibly only be six bears left in the world. Just because there were only eight on that ice floe, doesn't mean there are only six left. There are probably others out there. You just can't see them because they camouflage with the snow. You remember that word camouflage don't ya Mrs. Davis, because you taught us it.*

My youngest son came home from school one day in second grade bursting with important news. I was on the phone and despite my raised 'wait' finger he really wanted me to know what he had to say, so he grabbed a paper and pencil and wrote me a note. It said, "*in mi spelin test tuda i gut evre wun rit aksept wun.*" Both the teacher and parent in me were bursting with pride at that moment. I posted the note on the staff lounge fridge the next day along with a thank you note to his teacher.

Grammar is a tricky thing for kids, but spelling gives us teachers no end of entertainment. This is not limited to just the little guys, although the best creations come from them. One of my first graders labeled her science notebook as *Gwen's Sins Book*. Seriously, how much sin does a six-year-old have to record? Another child in that same first grade class reported in his journal that he liked porn. I think he meant corn... I hope he meant corn. My all-time favourite was from a first grader who attended a church called *Focus on the Family*. When asked to write about what her family does on the weekend she wrote, "We go f**k on the flamly."

Often Kinder spelling is based on the child's own pronunciation of the word. One day we were brainstorming words that start with qu. One of my sporty little boys who rarely contributed during literacy lessons shot his hand in the air. When I called on him he jumped up and mimed hitting a ball with a cricket bat as he yelled, "Quicket!"

One way to work out what a child is trying to say when using 'invented spelling' is to think Icelandic. When we visited Iceland I was intrigued with the length of the words. Eyjafjallajökull is one of the most famous volcanoes in Iceland, but you will never be able to ask anybody where it is, because if you are not a native Icelander you can't say it. Then there is Vatnajökull (glacier), which is a little easier. By the time you get to Dyngjujökull (the icecap on another glacier), you are beginning to see a pattern at the end and surmise that *kull* may have something to do with ice.

Thankfully one of the locals explained to us that the Icelandic language has changed very little since Viking times and many of the words were actually phrases. This helped with our efforts. A word with seventeen consonants and only five vowels might actually mean 'a sturdy little horse with a brown mane and a foul temper'.

So, ever since that enlightening conversation I go all Icelandic with my brain when encountering invented spelling and think *phrase* rather than *word* and it pops right out at you, like one of my favourites: losenlosuv. When I asked this particular fledgling writer to translate losenlosuv for me she said, "You know, Mrs. Davis. It's an old-fashioned expression to describe *a really lot of something* – you know – *lots and lots of*." Ohhh... I get it now.

What follows is a short introductory guide to first grade spelling. These are the *actual* spellings of words and phrases that I have jotted down from student work over the years. These days teachers call it invented spelling and in the spirit of not squashing enthusiasm for early learners it is encouraged. We used to call it *wrong* when I was in elementary school, but gosh darn it I was a good invented speller.

Cover up the words on the right in the samples below and try reading these gems. Go full-on phonetic and say it exactly as it is written and you have a fighting chance of deciphering the meaning.

Axudently = accidentally
Banuka = brand new car
Beste Tererr = best teacher
Bihavyr = behaviour
Butefol = beautiful

Chrash = trash

Ciweshtens = questions

Cwestins = questions

Folode = followed

Froshuzdinosrkloz = ferocious dinosaur claws

Gamuanganpuzhowz = grandma and grandpa's house

Gointusokrpraktiz = going to soccer practice

Gratis techr = greatest teacher

Hlareis = hilarious

Inahaf = and a half

Ixsrmle = extremely

Jinomisle = gianormously

Jravwoae = driveway

Juraf = giraffe

Konstrokshonwrkr = construction worker

Kwestins = questions

Losenlosuv = lots and lots of

Luct = looked

Makuroneanteez = macaroni and cheese

Masbutatos = mashed potatoes

Misdrpebode = Mr. Peabody

Noktrnol = nocturnal

Nolijibl = knowledgeable

Peeeanmusik = PE and music

Piyner = pioneer

Plesofser = police officer

Prizupolzofis = principal's office

Quiket = cricket

Raskarjriver = race car driver

Ridentuskulbuz = riding the school bus

Srtefuket = certificate

Shitr = sister

Shointel = show and tell

Spekinuv = speaking of

Shriemlee = extremely

Socasis = suitcases

Techer, techr, teatre, teechur, tesher = additional spellings for teacher

Ugen= again

Uv = of

Skuwel= school

Wunzuponutim = once upon a time

Yustoo = used to

Sometimes the actual misspelled words are not hard to figure out but there is a serious shift in the meaning. Take this sentence written by a nine-year-old boy explaining that the classmate sitting in front of him is his cousin. 'I am cusends with Amber that *shits* rite in front of me'. She does?

In kindergarten the very idea of reading and writing can sometimes seem mystical and elusive to the kids. Recently one of my kindergarteners finished writing his version of some sentences on a whiteboard. Delighted with himself, he dashed up to me and plopped it in my lap. "Read it to me please," he implored.

These are the exact lines he had written:

HETAMiTTiAE

HEAToEOETdiM

AEHALtEiM

I smiled encouragingly and invited him to read it to me instead. He stared at me like I was insane and declared. "*I* don't know what it says. *You're* the one who knows how to read."

Advice on spelling:

1. Consider using the deciphering of student writing as a great party game.

And That Just Happened! (AKA the Teachable Moment)

All teachers love it when a 'teachable moment' presents itself. These of course, are those rare and marvellous moments when something unexpected happens that just lends itself perfectly to teaching a lesson without any preplanning at all.

One day I was teaching my little first graders about observation. We had the classroom door open, because it was a very hot autumn day. This particular school in Colorado was built in the early 70s when buildings were no longer built with windows that opened or ceiling fans, but not yet the era where they installed air conditioning. So the only way to cool down on hot days was to prop the door open. This left us wide open to passing wildlife like bears, coyotes, etc.

On this particular day the wildlife came in the form of a fuzzy little bee. A bee in a classroom full of six and seven-year-olds may as well be a circus elephant for the excitement it generates. That tiny buzzing insect came zipping in and started pinging off the walls and dive-bombing my screaming class.

In an attempt to restore serenity, I waved my arms gently in long sweeping gestures as I implored them to calm down. "If you don't hurt her, she won't hurt you," I sagely advised. As I brought my arms back down the sneaky little bugger zoomed straight in and stung my inner arm just above the elbow. I looked at the stunned faces of my little pupils and uttered something like, "Oh, golly gee. That bee just stung me. Shucks."

In the interest of seizing the teachable moment, I decided we could 'observe' the changes in my arm. The students were fascinated to watch the growing red lump. "Well, gosh darn it, will you look at that," I crooned as the angry lump transformed before their very eyes into a fifth appendage.

My more studious little urchins grabbed their science notebooks and began to make sketches that looked like sausages. Several of the students decided they needed to use their sense of touch to explore this fascinating phenomenon. "Whoa, Mrs. Davis, it's really hot!" they exclaimed.

"Poor little bee. It's going to die now ya-know," one of my know-it-alls announced. That little scientist is lucky my sausage arm didn't accidentally twitch into his face.

The very next day on the playground, one of the girls from the class decided to employ Mrs. Davis' mellow strategy of bee taming with similar end results.

Playground tricks are a great launching point for lessons in rudimentary physics. Every school that I have ever taught at has some form of monkey bars. Every school also has a Hannah Helpful who grabs her panicking little friend around the ankles while soothing, "It's OK. You can let go now. I got ya." No, honey – you don't.

As soon as the trusting child lets go of the bars the laws of physics take over and unless the child being 'saved' has incredible abdominal development (not a hallmark of primary students) or has had advanced circus training, gravity takes over and the upper half of the body, with feet still firmly held by the soon to be un-friended one, heads for the ground. If the kids are roughly the same size this results in a rather high-speed collision of the face with the ground. Often the would-be hero is left holding the shoes, as their former friend spits out dirt and teeth. Physics 101.

Crickets, just FYI, do not leave their shipping container in an orderly fashion. In first grade we populated our carefully prepared terrariums with pill bugs and crickets. The crickets came from a science supply company in little cylindrical cardboard containers. The first year we did this nobody had told me that it is best to refrigerate the crickets for a couple of hours before opening the lid. This cold treatment slows them down a bit.

Because this bit of information was not shared with me, I prepped the kids and then with great ceremony opened the top of the container to distribute said crickets. Pandemonium ensued as crickets populated every corner of the room within about three seconds. Some took up residence in the classroom air vent and entertained us for many weeks to follow with their incessant chirping.

The science lesson learned here was that crickets survive much better in metal air vents without food or water than they do in carefully prepared terrariums. They also survived in the containers that had the lids clapped back on them before they could escape. We discovered this fact well over a month later. The crickets survived by eating the paper inside the container. Fascinating what one can learn from unexpected events.

Weather provides the very best of the, "Well, that just happened," moments. One delightful spring day in the foothills of the Colorado Rockies at T-minus ten minutes to dismissal time a wild hailstorm descended on our humble little school. One moment the kids were stacking their chairs and getting ready to go get their backpacks out of the hallway and the next moment dark descended and they were covering their ears and cowering in fear as hailstones the size of bowling balls (well, maybe grapes) pummelled the window.

One tiny girl began to wail and that set off a chain reaction of bawling that would rival any tragic scene of fear and dismay ever to fill a TV screen. The principal came over the PA and announced that nobody was to leave the school building to walk home or go to buses until the storm had passed. We were to keep all kids in the classrooms. Now we had full-blown panic.

In order to soothe their fears, I called them all down to the rug to calm them down. I said – and I quote, "OK.

Everybody take a deep breath and calm down. I know it is extremely loud and kind of scary, but you are safe. You are inside a building and hail *can't hurt you inside a building.*" As the din reduced to a few sniffles and those clinging to one another slowly loosened their grip I sent them out to the hallway to grab their coats and backpacks. OK. Good. Now we were all calmer and the ringing in my ears had begun to subside.

Suddenly, my frantic students dashed back into the room with their hands covering their heads as if bombs were raining from the sky shrieking, "The hail is hitting us in the head. It is coming out from the vents!" What? It's what? Sure enough, hail was spewing from the cold air return vents out in the hallway. How, you ask? How should I know? Some kind of weird phenomena involving billiard ball type angles and secret passages in the ceiling space I suppose. Whatever it was, I had just lied to a bunch of six and seven-year-olds. Flat out lied. Hail *can* hurt you inside a building. Lesson learned – the teacher has no idea what she is talking about.

Early on in my teaching career I was walking past a classroom that was clearly out of control. Who was I as a fledgling teacher to question another teacher's methods? Something about this was different though. Kids were screeching and the teacher was yelling, "Get back! Get back!" Pausing outside the door, I thought to myself, "*Self,* perhaps you should just go in and have a look."

I entered to a chaotic scene. A geyser of water was shooting out of the sink towards the ceiling as the teacher futilely tried to block it with a wad of paper towels. She was panicky, so the kids were panicky. This situation needed some calm. I sidled over to the frantic teacher and asked, "Why don't you just shut the water off?"

She glared at me and yelled, "What?" as if she were trying to be heard over Niagara Falls.

"Just shut the water off," I repeated as I reached under the sink and shut the water off at the wall.

Thrown off by the sudden end to the drama, the frazzled teacher sat down on the nearest chair and whispered, "I didn't know you could do that." Well you can. Every water source has a shut off valve. Teachable moment.

Teachable moments can be staged, however this is not a recommended course of action. Kids are too savvy and they may see through it. It is better just to leave it to the inevitable result if you have given them enough warning. Every year somebody learns the hard way that there is wisdom in the teacher's plea to not tip back in your chair and balance on just the two back legs. Do not run on the ice is also a valuable bit of advice. Bits of advice like these are not internalized until somebody has cracked the back of their head in full view of the rest of the class.

My advice on teachable moments:

1. Do not stage a teachable moment. They will come to you.
2. Try to embrace the moment, even if it is painful.
3. Don't worry if you didn't seize the moment. There will be more.

Shining Moments

Shining moments for me are those glorious incidents when children who are not the future cheerleaders or class presidents have their moment in the sun. These are often the geeky little kids with crooked glasses frames, no muscle tone, unkempt hair, and perhaps a little snot continually running out of their nose. They have a lot to offer the world, but it will happen in their own time and most likely behind the scenes.

Back in my PE days I taught a little boy who not only had no muscle tone, but most definitely had no aptitude or desire in the athletic arena. Unfortunately, he *did* care that he stood out as the slowest, most uncoordinated and least likely to contribute to team success. One tremendously windy day in Colorado Springs his third grade class was practicing throwing Frisbees for distance in preparation for our upcoming Field Day. He had repeatedly thrown his Frisbee directly into the ground at his feet.

On about his four hundred and ninety-eight attempt to get the darn thing airborne a freak gust of wind grabbed his Frisbee and sent it soaring the length of the soccer field. Frozen with disbelief, he was knocked over by a congratulatory smack on the back by Mr. Future

Quarterback, who was so amazed at this unexpected performance by a classmate he had never even noticed before, that he enthusiastically shouted that his 'best friend' had just won!

Shining moments don't have to be monumental to be notable. As I was reading to the kids one afternoon, a moth was fluttering around my rocking chair. Distracting as this was, I doggedly read on until one little guy sitting at my feet suddenly reached up with both hands and seized that little bugger with lightning quick speed. He then released the moth outside to the cheers of his future Greenpeace classmates. This is not so outstanding in and of itself, but he repeated the procedure not two minutes later with a large fly, snatching it out of the air with one hand as it zoomed past a classmate's ear. This is all it takes in the world of six-year-olds to have superhero status.

My all-time favourite shining moment occurred one day as my first graders were returning to class from recess. The little girl I introduced earlier in this book as the Phoenix was engaged in a heated argument with the class kingpin. In an effort to diffuse what was about to get physical I asked what the problem was. Kingpin snapped, "Phoenix claims she can talk to birds... and they talk to her... and nobody can talk to birds like that."

I calmly replied, "Well, maybe she can."

Emboldened by my belief in her superpower, Phoenix pointed to an oversized crow on the roof of the school, then spread her scrawny arms like powerful wings and bellowed, "Caw, caw, caw!" The bird turned to face Phoenix, spread its wings in the exact same way and replied, "Caw, caw, caw!" in a perfect duplication of Phoenix's tone and inflection.

Stunned, some of the class dropped to their knees in prayer, as others began to gather around our little bird whisperer in admiration. Beaming, Phoenix slowly turned in a full circle with her hands raised in the air in a victory pose. Thereafter, half the class played birds with Phoenix at recess and even Kingpin had to grudgingly show a cautious sort of respect for her obvious super power.

I live for shining moments. Many of them are not really the sorts of stories that make it into a book. They are those tiny personal moments when a child realises their own potential or affirms their self worth. Watch for them and relish them.

The Secret to Teaching Real Kids

Now that you know what it is like to teach real kids, at least from my perspective, you might be wondering how and why I still teach. Or maybe not, since I said at the start of this book that the reason I still teach is that the kids make me laugh every day. That is true, but how I manage to do that is with love. The big secret to continue enjoying teaching through trial and tribulation, calamity and triumph, is *love and laughter*.

Love the children. Hug them when they need it. Wipe their tears. Laugh at their lame jokes. Praise effort more than achievement. Feed them when they have had no breakfast. Buy them gloves when their hands are cold every day. Listen when nobody else will. Care. See the world through their eyes. Laugh with them. But most importantly – love them when they are least loveable.

Parting Words

When I thought I was going to retire (which didn't happen) I asked my first graders to each give me just one bit of advice. The advice I got fit nicely into two distinct categories. About half were fairly solid practical suggestions like: go to Disneyland, go swing at the park, play at the beach or go on a trip. The other suggestions were truly inspiring.

To my delight, and fuelling my already well developed imagination, the kids gave me some fantastic new ideas such as: fly on a pterodactyl, battle a gorilla, capture a dragon, ride a T-Rex, live in a bat cave, or be a ninja. I have to admit that at sixty-years-old I was flattered that the kids saw me as capable of such amazing feats.

Due to my young students' unequivocal belief in me and their zest for life and all its infinite possibilities, I hesitated only briefly when just two weeks after moving back to Australia and blissfully slipping into my semi-retired status of casual relief teaching, I was offered a full time position on a year four class. I toured the school with the principal, met a couple of young characters along the way and was hooked back in. And so it goes. I teach on.

As I said at the beginning of this book, I will most likely continue to teach either in my own classroom or as a casual relief teacher until I can no longer see the humour in a fart. My challenge to my fellow teachers is to summon the enthusiasm to teach and genuinely love their little charges every day with vigour, spontaneity and joy. Allow young students' imaginations to take flight! Good luck, my friends, and whatever happens, remember to laugh!

Teach on!